C000203215

'This book doesn't just contain a who
mind, breath, eyes, ears and hands.
Kerry Thorpe, but the heart, mind, e
work within and through his church, turning us inside out for the
sake of the world he loves. Enjoyably engaging, deeply practical and
personally challenging.'
Justin Welby, Archbishop of Canterbury

'This is a superb guide – easy to read, vivid, biblically well-grounded,
widely informed and immensely practical.'
Revd Dr Michael Moynagh, Wycliffe Hall, Oxford

'Cracking stuff – grounded, practical, inspirational and passionate.
It's made me want to go and find an accompanier for myself!'
Canon Lucy Moore, Messy Church Team Leader BRF

'Kerry Thorpe, as the leading person in this area, has something
vital to share with the church about mission accompaniment. His
experience personally and as a church and diocesan leader means
he has lived this book for the last 40 years.'
Revd Canon Dave Male, National Advisor for Pioneer Development

'Kerry Thorpe writes about what he has spent a lifetime doing. He
has read widely and reflects honestly on success and failure. In an
over-optimistic, self-promoting, goal-driven managerial culture
that has entered parts of the church, I'm delighted Kerry writes out
of seeing life and coaching in relational terms. So, he knows and
describes coaching techniques, but holds them lightly. The book
combines an easy style and deep insights.'
Canon Dr George Lings, formerly Director of the Church Army's Research Unit, Sheffield

The Bible Reading Fellowship
15 The Chambers, Vineyard
Abingdon OX14 3FE
brf.org.uk

The Bible Reading Fellowship (BRF) is a Registered Charity (233280)

ISBN 978 0 85746 595 5
First published 2018
10 9 8 7 6 5 4 3 2 1 0
All rights reserved

Acknowledgements
Unless otherwise acknowledged, scripture quotations are taken from The Holy
Bible, New International Version (Anglicised edition) copyright © 1979, 1984, 2011
by Biblica. Used by permission of Hodder & Stoughton Publishers, a Hachette UK
company. All rights reserved. 'NIV' is a registered trademark of Biblica. UK trademark
number 1448790.

Extracts from the Authorised Version of the Bible (The King James Bible), the rights
in which are vested in the Crown, are reproduced by permission of the Crown's
Patentee, Cambridge University Press.

Scripture quotations from the Good News Bible published by The Bible Societies/
HarperCollins Publishers Ltd, UK © American Bible Society 1966, 1971, 1976, 1992,
used with permission.

Every effort has been made to trace and contact copyright owners for material used
in this resource. We apologise for any inadvertent omissions or errors, and would
ask those concerned to contact us so that full acknowledgement can be made in
the future.

A catalogue record for this book is available from the British Library

Printed and bound by CPI Group (UK) Ltd, Croydon CR0 4YY

a guide to mission accompaniment

Kerry M. Thorpe

BRF

Contents

Introduction: discovering relational accompaniment

Setting up the engagement

Here is yet another book that could change your life! This time with the added bonus that it could also materially impact your church, your workplace, your diocese, your family and your friends. This book invites you to a journey. Together, we could significantly affect the quality of our living and working environments. Whether you are a professional coach wanting to be more effective in enhancing performance, or a colleague wanting to facilitate greater flourishing, or simply a friend wanting to be of greater value, making a bigger difference for those you love, here is an opportunity to explore.

So, first an opening question: what are you hoping for?

What single, clarified outcome would best repay time spent invested in reading this book? Put your answer into actual, specific words. Then ask yourself: what would that do for me? How might I be different if I actually achieved that aim? In what ways could my life and ministry be enhanced? Who might I be able to serve better? Who could I personally invest in, with what I have discovered here?

This book is an invitation to explore relational accompaniment together. I suggest that the whole experience will work best if we treat it as an actual accompaniment. See this as an engagement over however long it takes for you to read (and possibly reread) this book. I invite you to bring your own story to the table and take time, genuinely, to respond to what might otherwise seem like rhetorical questions. Be specific, make notes, keep a journal, perhaps. Take the risk of setting out, not entirely sure of the destination, but with a deep willingness to end up somewhere fresh and unfamiliar. That way, we can model together, incarnate the principles and try out the practices that are laid out here.

As the author, I will need to share something of my own story. This will serve as both introduction to, and exploration of, some of the key principles in our relational accompaniment journey. It will, of necessity, be rather personal.

The mother of invention

I had no idea what to do. It felt overwhelming. I don't think I had any illusions about full-time ministry being a bed of roses, but this was way beyond anything that I had anticipated. Like so many of my colleagues before and since, I found myself asking if I had in any way been adequately prepared for what I now faced. Life, never mind ministry, makes demands. It is an inescapable component of the human condition to find ourselves confronted by challenges that look to be hopelessly beyond our capabilities. This, for me, was where the story of relational accompaniment starts.

I had spent four years in theological college. Previously riding racehorses for a living and later qualifying as an embalmer in the funeral trade had taught me much about life (and its opposite). Now I had a degree in theology to add to the resources. This was my first curacy, and a role as a junior member of a large staff team in as busy a parish church as could be found in the late 1970s. One thousand people per week came through the doors to services, community events and children's work that spanned all ages. My specific responsibility was for the teenagers. There was already a flourishing group, between 20 and 50 strong, that well predated my arrival.

Now the vicar had taken ill. Roy Barker, the much-loved man in charge, was no longer on the scene. After 18 years of transforming mission, the team leader and driving force was suddenly absent. This was the unanticipated crisis in what already looked like a massive challenge. It was clearly going to be all hands on deck. The remaining four full-time staff would have to share out responsibilities. The neat division of labour so far envisaged would be shot to pieces. Much more would be needed of us. (No one knew how long this was going to last. In the event, the vicar was ill for about a year. Then he announced a move and the parish was in interregnum. Finally, a new appointment was made, and quite naturally the new man needed adequate time to discern his own priorities. All in all, the situation continued for about three years.) This was going to be not so much a crisis, more a way of life.

So, how could we continue to see growth? How would we conserve the gains already made? Or, more realistically, how might we even survive?

For me, the great insight that would urge me on through the next 40 years of ministry was born not out of a deeply spiritual season of prayer and discernment, nor out of a highly structured management planning session, but out of crisis, out of sheer desperation.

The only sustainable way forward that I could envisage would need other people, many other people. If they had already known what to do, then presumably they would have been doing it by now. This was going to require some fresh thinking. It would mean breaking new ground and many of us doing what we had not previously imagined. More people involved, more gifts harnessed, new skills developed and old reluctance and barriers overcome.

From where would this amazing army of volunteers emerge? How could we recruit, train, develop and support a brand-new tranche of effective leaders? The answer was quite simply that we couldn't. That would be a dream too far. We would have to work with what we had already got. And that was it. That was the breakthrough.

My main responsibility was for that blossoming group of teenagers. They were of course as remarkable, capable, trying, disruptive and annoying as any bunch of kids that you might wish to meet. Within the pack were some natural leaders. There were others who might be encouraged to develop those gifts. There were kids with bright ideas and some who could just as easily be trouble. They were capable of great disruption, or perhaps they were young adults just waiting to blossom. Either way, they were potential on legs.

Sheer survival determined that there would be little time to run anything like a selection process for what lay ahead. My wife and I, with two other couples from the congregation to help, sat down with our list of teenage participants. We prayed, of course we prayed. Then we simply divided up the list into groups, using our scant knowledge of personalities and proclivities. Within each group we identified a potential peer-group leader. For each leader we nominated an associate from within that same group. To each group we allocated one of the adult couples as support. And so, for us, the concept of relational mission accompaniment was born. In effect, the teens themselves would do the ministry. They would run the small-group meetings. They would keep in touch with each other between times. We would provide the support. We could never have given adequate personal attention to a group of 50 or so youngsters, but we could, between us, help to develop significantly five or ten individuals. That is exactly what we did.

Lesson learned

This short, headline-grabbing story shows that three years later, those three groups of ten or twelve had grown to ten such units. The 30 to 50 had become somewhere around 100 plus. There were large-scale Sunday-evening gatherings for the whole crowd, but life, support, mission and growth happened in those smaller, peer-led, relational groupings. The adults focused almost entirely on supporting the young emerging leaders.

It must be stressed that this was not initially a strategy for growth. It was a bunch of fallible human beings adopting a high-risk approach in a bid for sheer survival. It laid the foundation for what I later discovered alluded to by William James, the founder of modern sociology and chronicler of spiritual experience:

> I am done with great things and big plans, great institutions and big success. I am for those tiny, invisible loving human forces that work from individual to individual, creeping through the crannies of the world like so many rootlets, or like the capillary oozing of water, which, if given time, will rend the hardest monuments of pride.[1]

There is, quite naturally, a mass of detail, trial and error, failure as well as success behind the headline story of our Merseyside youth work. But the principle holds absolutely firm. What could *not* have been achieved by a single individual became flourishing, sustainable mission and growth when more and more individuals were developed, supported and accompanied through their own burgeoning ministry. At the heart of it, the one individual whose story I am most qualified to tell escaped burnout, survived inordinate pressure and flourished. Giving ministry away, releasing the gifts and callings of other people and, above all, concentrating on a relational mission accompaniment was going to shape my approach to the multiplicity of missional challenges that the next 40 years would bring.

Delving deeper into the personal background

Like many of my post-war, baby-boom generation, I was introduced to Christian faith through Sunday school. Coloured stickers, simple stories and memorable songs provided a backdrop to growing up. As I progressed to Sunday-morning Matins in our tiny Saxon Sussex village church, the greatest challenge was trying to guess the exact number of minutes into the sermon that the organist would unwrap his first boiled sweet. It gave me a background in middle-class British cultural Christianity. What it didn't give me was any sort of preparation to negotiate the squally waters of growing up and facing the world.

When the first wave of crisis hit, in those troublesome teenage years, I turned to an old family friend, who had been responsible for children's work back in that rural parish church. An hour sitting, talking, listening and being listened to in his study provided as much if not more than all the previous hours spent in services added together. I didn't know it at the time, but a foundation of understanding was being laid. Was it counselling, mentoring, discipling or simple friendship? What does that matter? It was personal, relational, developmental and life-transforming. Without being overtly conscious of it, I was acquiring the core values of mission accompaniment.

Living the values

Going back to that first Merseyside curacy, I was building on foundations long since laid. As a staff team in a leaderless church, we quickly learned how best to support each other. As a leader team with responsibility for a bunch of teenagers, we discovered that by working with and walking with the key youngsters, then our work could be multiplied. The lads and girls whom we accompanied in turn accompanied others, and the work grew. It ruined me for a traditional evangelical parish-church ministry of trying to pack the pews by powerful preaching. From now on, mission would be shaped by the values of relational accompaniment.

More grist to the mill

During the 1970s and 80s, there was a developing awareness of church growth theory and practice in the British church. Most of the models came from overseas, and particularly from across the Atlantic. There was a ready acknowledgement that the church in the

UK needed to get its act together, but an understandable suspicion that practices developed elsewhere would not easily translate into our context. I found myself teaching church growth in a variety of settings and to a range of denominations. If, like William James before me, I was 'done with great things and big plans', how was I going to champion an emphasis on growth?

Having babies versus raising the dead: insight from church planting

The next phase of ministry took me into the realms of church planting. Three years of work in the parish of Chester-le-Street, County Durham, is told in the 1984 MARC Europe publication *Ten Growing Churches*. One parish, six church plants, using what became known as the 'strawberry runner' model of planting; this allowed for growth not by getting big at the centre, but by sending out and supporting teams across the town. 'It's easier to have babies than to raise the dead' was an aphorism that I think I picked up later from John Wimber. Whatever its provenance, the sentiment is clear. Nationally, the church needed a fresh start, new thinking, models of mission that were about more than packing pews. There was still no fully formed understanding of relational mission accompaniment at work here, but it is clear to me now that this was the underlying value of this growth. I was working a second curacy, overseeing one of the plants and coordinating more than 30 home-based groups around the parish, all under the leadership of the incumbent, Ian Bunting. 'I am more interested in growing big people than big congregations' was another of those aphorisms whose exact origin escapes me, but clearly informed all that we were about.

Building from scratch – almost

After I had worked on the staff team of two churches whose congregations numbered, at their peak, around 1,000 people per week, it was a bit of a shock to pick up a first incumbency in a parish church with a congregation of 30. St George's, Fatfield had been built at the end of the 19th century to serve a small County Durham mining community. By 1984, the year of my arrival and of the infamous pit closures, the village had been subsumed into Washington New Town. The tiny congregation had been pastored and loved over the years and were now ready for growth. 'Please come and help to lead us into the future,' they said. Who could refuse?

Several years later, the story ran in several national papers, and led to an interview with Michael Parkinson. On 29 May 1991, *The Sun* put it like this: 'Vicar Kerry Thorpe has boosted his church's flock by a hundred-fold – by fitting fancy furniture.'

The reality was rather different, but who am I to contradict our beloved tabloid press? The following day *The Times* ran it this way: 'Congregations have risen from thirty to three hundred at St George's Church, Washington, Tyne & Wear, since the Rev Kerry Thorpe installed spotlights, comfortable chairs and pink carpets.'

The press missed the point, but the concept of relational accompaniment was growing. Help individuals to flourish; grow the people. Anyone who was part of that Fatfield story would know that most of the real work was done by others. It was Pat and Maurice and Kate, Elizabeth and Rodney, Dave and Bob. I didn't, and don't, have the gifts or the skills to achieve those kinds of results. Of course, it was God, but God working through growing people, who were more than capable of transforming their own community given the vision, encouragement and support. Still, I can't deny that I enjoyed my moment in '*The Sun*'.

The road to Canterbury

Drawing on all that had gone before, the concept of relational mission accompaniment finally took shape for me in the years that I have worked for the Diocese of Canterbury. Initially, in 1993, as vicar of Holy Trinity, Margate, my task was to oversee the planting of St Philip's Church on the Northdown Park Estate. This was a purpose-built new church set among new housing. So far, so normal. But beyond that comes the story of resigning parish ministry and planting HARVEST New Anglican Church, which was a forerunner of the Fresh Expressions movement.[2]

The grit in the oyster

Despite all the foregoing accounts of flourishing ministry (and doesn't it look good when only summarised and edited?), there was an equally important lesson to be drawn from failure. The planting of HARVEST, and the subsequent focus on accompanying and developing individuals, finally took shape because of my incapacity to hold it all together at parish-church level. I had not managed to carry the confidence of the regular congregation at Holy Trinity, the parent church. It was my inability to manage the demands of a large and lively church at the same time as growing a new congregation that finally led to the definitive leap of faith that became HARVEST. Only by almost being crushed under the demands of parish-church administration did I finally clarify a conviction to do church differently, or not at all. I had no idea that I was 'part of a movement'. Once again, I simply thought that I was trying to survive.

Ironically, having spent my first 30 years of ministry moving further and further out towards the edges of structured Church of England parish life, I have spent the last ten years working back at the centre. By 2006 it was recognised that the HARVEST experience, and the relational development at its heart, had something to contribute to the existing structures of the diocese. Since then I have worked as Fresh Expressions Missioner, and subsequently as Mission and Growth Advisor, across Canterbury Diocese and beyond. All the time, I was trying desperately to apply the principles of individual flourishing and relational accompaniment in a culture that appears at first sight to be oblivious to both.

Your personal reflection

There is a little of my own story. What now of yours?

- What are the influences that have helped to shape the person that you are becoming?
- Who are the people who have invested most deeply in your growth?
- What have you learned, to date, about relational accompaniment?
- When have you found yourself thinking, specifically, 'Is it just me, or is there a better way to be doing this?'

Take time to answer those questions. Risk some personal honesty, identify your own starting point, and then let's commit to making the next steps of the journey together.

1

The case for accompaniment

Imagine a world with everyone committed to lifelong learning about living well. Picture an environment in which you could flourish and then make a difference for your family and friends. Consider the possibility of contributing to a shift in culture for your colleagues and companions, in your church and your workplace. Prepare to embrace accompaniment.

The premise

Accompaniment is consistent engagement, with individuals or teams, for the greater flourishing of their lives and work. It will include elements of coaching, mentoring and simple friendship. It will reveal its greatest value as each of those elements is combined and transcended.

The principles and practices of accompaniment will be equally applicable at the start, the middle and the end of a journey of faith. They will make a significant contribution to discipling, to supporting ministry and to developing leadership roles. They will inform and enhance coaching, mentoring and indeed simple friendship. They will contribute to our flourishing in all that God has intended for us as friends and colleagues. They will make a difference for the kingdom of God.

I have been decorating the Christmas tree. Baubles, lights (whatever happened to tinsel?) and tiny gifts. The overall effect, I hope, will be one of wonder. How lovely! Doesn't that look pretty? What attractive lights. What delicate baubles. But at the heart of the overall effect is the tree, always the tree. No tree, no baubles. No tree, no lights. For all the eye-catching effect, it is always and ever dependent upon the tree.

In this story, relational accompaniment is the tree. Coaching and mentoring are the lights. Positive thinking and neuro-linguistic programming (NLP, more of each later) are the baubles. At heart, it is always about the tree. Good, solid, honest, godly, interpersonal relationship is the foundation for all that follows.

The shape of the journey

This chapter provides an outline of what is to come. Here is an overflight of the paths we are about to explore together. This is the lie of the land, the terrain we are about to traverse. Let's take a look at the shape of the journey before setting out to examine the detail.

We will, as a matter of principle, look first at theology. We want to remind ourselves of how the Christian tradition understands God. We then move on to look at psychology and popular contemporary understandings of human nature. Further on, we explore the relational nature of church. We take time to focus on the relational principles and practices at work in the ministry of Jesus. From there comes a description of coaching, and of one specific model now current within and beyond church circles. Beyond that will be a simple overview of the literature and language of NLP and of the constructive contribution that it can make.

In the latter half of the book, we will be introduced to some of the specifics of the Christian practice of accompaniment. There is a story to be told of missional thinking and its evolution from paternalism to accompaniment. There are anecdotes and glimpses of a practice that has been emerging, sometimes uncharted, during our lifetime. We will look at examples of how this has been worked out in relation to individuals, to teams, to mission project coordinators and to senior church leaders.

Towards the end, a simple critique will be offered. We listen to our critics, who may accuse us of buying into a self-focused or materialistic drive towards greater productivity. We hold on to valuable insights to do with positivity, intentionality and purpose – we listen and learn.

By then, we will be ready to outline some of the practical principles of applied accompaniment. A simple model will be offered that can be mapped on to many of our engagements with colleagues, fellow disciples, family and friends. We can explore the difference that makes a difference.

Finally, there will be a refocusing on our ultimate goal. This is about a Christian desire to maintain orientation towards the nature and calling of God. Accompaniment is about taking seriously the delightful quotation from the second-century St Irenaeus of Lyon: 'The glory of God is [hu]mankind fully alive'.

Your personal reflection

Before moving on, ask yourself,

- What does that glory of God look like in practice?
- How might we enhance its development in one another?

Starting with God

In making the case for accompaniment, we will start at the beginning. Transforming friendship, we discover in chapter 2, is integral to God's nature. God walks with Eve and Adam in the garden. Later, he calls Abraham to be his friend (Isaiah 41:8). Jesus invites Galilean peasants to walk with him, and within that growing relationship he also describes them as his friends (John 15:15). Paul describes his, and subsequently all, Christian ministry in equally relational terms (2 Corinthians 5:19). Reconciliation, the mending of broken friendship, lies at the heart of Paul's ministry and the ministry that he commends to the next generation. The final fulfilment, depicted in the Revelation vision, is described in the phrase 'God himself will be with them' (Revelation 21:3). There is an unmistakable theme of walking with, journeying together and transformational friendship running all the way through the many biblical strands that are woven together to form Christian theology.

We will discover that inviting into and growing in relationship is foundational to the gospel. Journeying together is incarnated in both the message and the method. 'God invites your friendship' is the message. 'Jesus makes friends', we will see, is the method. He walks with us, we walk with each other and together we journey into the future. The ongoing post-biblical mission is described in exactly the same relational terms: 'so that you also may have fellowship with us. And our fellowship is with the Father and with his Son, Jesus Christ' (1 John 1:3). This is the theological underpinning of accompaniment spelled out in the early chapters. We change, we develop, we grow on the journey and we do it together in the company of those who love us and are committed to us.

Companions in literature

You need friends. Chapter 3 takes us from 'Relational God' to 'Relational human beings'. Even without access to a Bible, we would quickly reach this conclusion. 'There is nothing on this earth more to be prized than true friendship,' said Thomas Aquinas. (Whether his insight stemmed from personal experience or from study of scripture, history does not record.) Literature from all cultures down all ages explores that truth.

From the *Gilgamesh Epic*,[3] possibly the earliest recorded human story, comes a tale of companions, unlikely friendships and accompaniment through mystical and mythical lands. A markedly similar theme runs throughout J.R.R. Tolkien's *The Lord of the Rings*,[4] which has fired the imagination of many a journeying companion. Frodo is summoned, as an individual, to a personal quest. Despite his stubborn attempts, he discovers that he cannot achieve his destiny alone. He needs friends, and the kind of friends who 'stick closer than a brother': 'Go back, Sam! I'm going to Mordor alone.' 'Of course you are, and I'm coming with you!'

Friends will share the good times and the bad. Friends will love and support. Friends will guide and cajole. Friends will give honest feedback, swiftly dispel self-delusion and help us develop a realistic view of ourselves and our world. Friends help to bring out the best in us and together we can reach greater heights of fulfilment than are ever possible alone. None of us are self-sufficient, and none of us were ever meant to be. The relational nature of human beings, explored in chapter 3, will be developed as we delve further into the depths of relational accompaniment.

Learning from science

At our core, we are relational beings. Not only are theology, history and literature lined up in agreement over this, but recent neuroscience concurs. Our key developments take place in the context of our dealings with one another. We learn best in a relational context. Dan Siegel (professor of clinical psychiatry at UCLA) points out that the human brain developed the infrastructure for relationship ahead of its awaking to self-awareness.[5] The implication of that insight is that we need others in order to be truly ourselves. Only within the context of relationship can we come to a true blossoming of selfhood. It becomes clearer, as we progress, what this means for our continued growth and flourishing.

Chapter 4, 'Relational church', explores our calling to accompanied living. In an ideal world where all our deepest needs were being met, a consistent level of supportive, developmental relationship would simply be a description of the way things are. Family, friends and colleagues would be in a continual relationship of mutual development. Sadly, reality is not often like that. The gospel of restored relationship with a relational God draws us into a network of restored relationships with each other. God has set his heart on having a community of people who demonstrate that to the world.

This is why we are learning how to identify the need, develop the skills and offer the service of accompaniment to one another. This is the concept of relational accompaniment that informed the planting of HARVEST New Anglican Church, and so that story is related, as an exploration of these principles in practice, in chapter 4.

Learning from Jesus

Chapter 5 takes us into the Gospel accounts. Jesus needs friends: 'Couldn't you men keep watch with me for one hour?' (Matthew 26:40). Jesus makes friends: 'Jesus loved Martha and her sister and Lazarus' (John 11:5). Jesus commissions friend-making friends: 'Go, then, to all peoples everywhere' (Matthew 28:19, GNT). If God is relational, the gospel is relational and Jesus' own ministry is overwhelmingly relational, then the concept of relational accompaniment has solid theological foundations.

On to the world of coaching

What many of us have concluded theologically has been embraced pragmatically in the secular world. The desirability of mentoring relationships is increasingly recognised, not least in the sporting and commercial worlds. Coaches abound. Working with people one-on-one to aid development and performance is now big business. No aspiring athlete, of any discipline, would dream of seeking success without the aid of a coach. When a world-ranking tennis player hires a new coach, it makes sporting headlines. When performance dips, speculation over a new coaching appointment begins. 'I owe everything to my coach,' says a gold medal-winning athlete, gymnast, swimmer, diver, fencer or martial arts practitioner.

It proved to be a small step from sport to the world of business. Access to personal and business coaching is now a prerequisite for many an aspiring executive. How to maximise potential? How to gain an edge? How to identify and transcend personal self-limiting beliefs and behaviours? Call the coach.

Coaching goes beyond sport and business. It is not unusual for individuals wanting to develop their potential and to further their goals to call on the services of a life coach. The online 'Life Coach Directory' suggests that there are currently more than 100,000 life coaches offering their services worldwide. At the time of the publication of Laura Berman Fortgang's *Take Yourself to the Top* in 1998,[6] she listed just five points of contact in the UK. Growth industry, or what?

In recent days, the trend has come full circle (if we think that mentoring friendships started with God's purposes for humankind). Grove Books (Pastoral Series 115) is entitled *Coaching in the Church*.[7] The authors, Huw Thomas (a head teacher) and Martyn Snow (now Bishop of Leicester), make a case for adopting some simple coaching practices in order to develop the potential of ministerial colleagues.

No controversy, then, over the existence of coaching and developmental accompaniment, or its value and recent history. Chapter 6, 'Relational coaching', takes us more deeply into that world and explores its current use in church life, and how it can contribute to the wider concept of relational accompaniment.

The murky world of NLP

Two thousand pairs of eyes were focused on a massive screen showing a close-up of my face. It was meant to be a celebratory family night out at a London theatre, but somehow Derren Brown, the illusionist whose show this was, had picked me out. He had me standing up, and was attempting to read my mind, in front of a packed audience. He succeeded, obviously (that's show business), but it was a trick; of course, it was a trick. Derren Brown has helped to popularise the concept of NLP (neuro-linguistic programming), which he claims plays a part in his presentations. He has simultaneously raised questions about its authenticity and acceptability because of his love of what he calls 'misdirection'. Chapter 7, 'Relational accompaniment: developing individuals', looks to lift NLP out of the world of theatre and explore how the very real insights at its heart can actually be of enormous help in stimulating life-changing insight. Prepare to be convinced!

Past history and recent developments

Back in 2007, Churches Together in Britain & Ireland (CTBI) published a short booklet entitled *Journey into Growth*.[8] It told the story of their Building Bridges of Hope project, which they had run across three phases, starting twelve years earlier in 1995. CTBI had conducted research across denominations and throughout the British Isles. Their central conclusion was that 'a willingness to be accompanied' was at the heart of a flourishing missional life. The healthiest churches were accompanied churches. CTBI wanted to learn from the research and to discover if its findings could be replicated. They therefore proceeded to recruit and train a team of accompaniers, to test out their findings. Then they identified a range of Christian communities willing to participate in the experiment, so that they could research the outcomes more fully.

Accompaniers were matched with projects and set to work, visiting the leaders of their allocated congregations every couple of months over a four-year period. The final phase of the project was a concluding piece of research into the value of the accompaniment experience and the ongoing missional health of the projects themselves. Finally, the findings were published as *Journey into Growth*.

My first-hand experience of this work comes from being one of those who were accompanied. The story is told in greater detail in chapter 8, 'Relational accompaniment: the honing of an idea'. The small-group network-based Fresh Expressions of Church in which I was then pioneering was identified as a suitable pilot. HARVEST New Anglican Church had come into existence out of a desire to 'do church differently'.[9] Our accompanier, Tim Morgan (then working for Church Missionary Society), visited regularly, listened carefully, asked pertinent questions and reflected back honestly. We quickly learned to appreciate the value of a mission accompanier as a critical friend, a subtle questioner and a skilful companion.

Now here's a thing

Back in the 1980s, I had been recruited by Bible Society to work on their behalf as a teacher of church growth insights. Later, that role developed into a fully configured consultancy service offered to individual churches, Anglican deaneries, Methodist circuits and ecumenical groups of 'Churches Together'. For 20 years I fulfilled this role alongside my regular parish-church work. As my own ministerial circumstances changed over that time, I made a telling and surprising discovery: I was welcomed and received more readily and more warmly when I was coming from a small, struggling, humble, local church context than when I was perceived as arriving from the larger, more overtly successful setting. The penny dropped. Being listened to by someone who was perceived as understanding something of their ongoing struggles was of greater value than being told what to do by some bright spark from another planet. The pressing need was not actually for bright ideas, but for the accompanying friendship of an empathetic colleague. Hit-and-run consultancy was one thing; a friend for the journey was quite another.

In the years since 'Bridges of Hope', I have moved on to become an accompanier of others and a champion of the ongoing relational cause. Here in Canterbury Diocese, we have been trying to learn from best practice. As a result, we have gone on to offer our own version of coaching or mentoring, specifically developed and recast as accompaniment, in a variety of contexts. That is the story explored more deeply in chapter 9.

Three questions were being asked in different departments of diocesan life:

- How can we resource our pioneering 'Fresh Expressions' projects, only just getting off the ground and in need of love and nurture?
- What might we do to enable a greater likelihood of change and growth in the struggling parishes that have been identified as 'missionally challenging' and where grant money was being made available?
- And how could the diocese extend the reach of its central resource team? That is, how could diocesan officers, each with their own particular speciality, offer more support and make more of an impact on the churches within their care?

The answer in every case was to be 'accompaniment'. The outworking would be different. The core values and principles would be the same. This is the story to be told in chapter 9, 'Relational accompaniment: changing a culture'.

The relational heartbeat

Personal support for load-bearing individuals and the teams of which they are a part lies at the heart of the Canterbury story. We will hear how the strategy developed, was implemented and continues, relationally. It is a story of working with inherited structures, deaneries, benefices and parishes, as well as with the pioneering frontiers of Fresh Expressions of Church.

In every case, the presence of a mission accompanier helps to focus outwards and to ensure that mission informs every other decision. The accompanier does not have to be an expert, but does try to bring an independent perspective, ask pertinent questions and offer a connection to the wider diocesan story.

All told, this represents a bold attempt to change a culture through relational accompaniment. By emphasising 'journeying with' and learning together, we aim to shift the focus from survival to flourishing. That is the case for accompaniment made in chapter 9.

The challenge

As a matter of integrity, chapter 10 is called 'Relational accompaniment: learning from the critics'. There is understandably some discussion about the applicability of secular coaching or NLP principles to spiritual life. There is a healthy scepticism about the ability of techniques that appear to have derived from the positive-thinking genre to effect lasting change. What, anyway, is the relationship between a desire for success, quantifiable outcomes and a theology that is focused on self-giving and a life of service?

We want to be honest. Our accompaniment aspires to a vision of growth and new frontiers in mission. But much of our current experience of ministry is about managing areas of decline. Growth seems far off for many. An agenda focused exclusively on measurable progress will be at odds with the lived experience of many of our colleagues. Life is tough for many of us. Can we face that fact, be thoroughly realistic and yet still hold fast to a dream of flourishing?

Any meaningful model of accompaniment will need to take cognisance of the whole picture. Can we learn from the insights of contemporary coaching without buying into the underlying materialistic, success-oriented worldview? I will argue that we can. Can we enhance our commitment to Christian discipleship by reflecting on recent developments in transpersonal psychology? I will claim that it is possible. Can we become more effective in helping to shape the life journeys of those around us by laying a firm theological foundation and then building on it? Can we pursue an inquisitive exploration of what is currently informing the study of personal development and press it into Christian service? I will engage with the critics and conclude that 'Yes we can!' See what you think.

Putting it into practice

By chapter 11, we are in a position to spell out some of the practical components of the accompaniment journey. It really matters that we have laid the foundations, drawn together the insights and weighed the challenges before committing ourselves to action. So don't read that chapter first.

(Oh, you're back. How did I know that you were going to do that?)

The ultimate goal: a surprising discovery

In chapter 12, 'Towards the goal of relational accompaniment', we aim to do what all good accompaniment should aspire to, and that is to clarify our outcomes. Jesus puts it this way: 'I have come that they may have life, and have it to the full' (John 10:10). The goal of relational accompaniment is nothing short of the fulfilment of God's purposes for his creation. It is the breaking in of tomorrow's kingdom to the present reality of today. It is the lived anticipation of resurrection life. It is the consummation of the inner yearning of every individual for the fulfilling of potential. It is the harmonising healing of that for which creation groans. It is the all-in-all of the final reign of Christ.

The Christian life has always and ever had that ultimate aspiration. The ability to live out future hope in present reality has always been what the power of the Spirit is about. The skill lies in keeping the candle aflame despite the gusts of quotidian experience. The prophetic tension that lies between outrageous aspiration and down-and-dirty reality is the very locus of relational accompaniment. We can do it together. We can't, and were never meant to, do it alone.

Here's the surprise. Whether we are talking about being a good friend to a neighbour way away from the church, or mentoring a bishop into her unfulfillable job description; whether we are addressing the discipleship journey of a dubiously sceptical beginner or coaching a church-planting mission priest on a new housing estate; whether we are simply helping an old friend make a tough decision or working with a pioneering team of evangelists – the principles are the same. It is the same relational accompanying DNA that runs throughout.

This is the calling and culture of the whole church. Mission, in the sense of inviting others into a life-enhancing relational journey with God, coaching a potential leader, mentoring a missionary or simply being there for a favoured friend, has but one essential core component: relational accompaniment.

That's the territory mapped out for the journey ahead. Let's see what's possible.

Your personal reflection

- What now are you most hoping for in following this story?
- How will you commit yourself to practising what you discover here?
- How do you most want to be different as a result of taking this journey?

2

Relational God

Starting with the nature of God

God wants to make friends. Meaningful relationship is the heart and soul of Christian theology. God building relationship with his friend Abraham is the controlling metaphor of the Old Testament. Jesus making friends is the foundational story of the gospel. Those friends inviting others into the same network of kingdom relationship is the heartbeat of subsequent Christian mission. It is all relational and it all flows from our understanding of a relational God.

In this chapter, I am aiming to lay a solid theological foundation for our understanding of a relational God, who invites humankind into relationship with himself. This is what shapes the biblical story. It is because God is relational by nature that the gospel has the particular shape that it does. From this insight comes all that follows on the priority of making, and being, friends. The concept of accompaniment has its roots in the nature of God. It is an irrevocable part of who we are and how we function. We need each other because that is both our origin and our destiny, derived from the nature of God himself.

Genesis 1—3 and the formational story

Back to the beginning, once more.

'Let us make mankind in our image' is the phrase that introduces the human story in Genesis 1:26. In a very short while, we will be looking at a picture of God strolling in the garden in the cool of the evening with his friends Adam and Eve. Before we get into that charming image, there is an even more fundamental point to be made.

Very many of the creation myths, sagas and stories that have been preserved from the earliest human cultures are highly dramatic. Beasts and monsters of unimaginable shape and size fight among themselves. Usually they are slain and dismembered by hero gods or offspring of gods, who mould their remains into the firmaments, continents and islands that constitute our planet. Karen Armstrong, in *A Short History of Myth*,[10] explains simply the background to many of these stories. Vastly greater detail can be found in Alexander Eliot's *The Universal Myths*.[11] Read against that colourful background, the Genesis account is quietly subdued, markedly different and almost certainly unique.

From the beginning, this is a relational story. Less hyperbolic and less dramatic than accounts from other cultures to be sure, it homes in on the place of humanity in the heart and mind of a creating God. This is our story. This is what we need to hear and know in order to locate ourselves in the world.

The underlying purpose of the Genesis account is to answer the heart cry of bewildered humankind. Who am I? Why am I here? To answer our deepest questions, however, we are initially pointed away from ourselves and towards the purposes of God. Here we are looking for the insights and the metaphors that will help us to make sense of ourselves, our origins, our purpose and our destiny. It turns out to be all about God. This is a story that starts with God and his passion for relationship. It is his call, and it reflects his nature.

'Let *us* make mankind in our image.' Christian theology suggests that from the outset God is, in the very essence of his being, already in a mutual relationship of three. The doctrine of the Trinity was not formulated in explicit terms until the early centuries of the Christian era. But, so the argument goes, that was only spelling out what had always been true. From the start, God exists as a harmony of loving relationship (what we later describe as Father, Son and Holy Spirit). Of course, this description does not provide scientifically verifiable information about the ultimate nature of reality. What it does is give us a picture, an image and a metaphor that will define and set boundaries to our exploration of God. Whichever way you look at it, God is irrevocably relational.

This then is the God who proceeds to say of the prototype being, 'it is not good for the man to be alone' (Genesis 2:18). Adam needs Eve. Clearly that is biologically necessary. It is also, in the context of the Genesis story, spiritually and psychologically necessary. 'Bone of my bones and flesh of my flesh' (Genesis 2:23). No gender-specific point-scoring here, just the simple insight that a relational God creates relational human beings. Here now are the couple who walk with each other and with God in the garden in the cool of the day. Perfect.

Many a slip

Like all gripping drama, Genesis 3 heightens the tension. The sense of jeopardy increases as the foundational perfection is lost. Paradise is lost in tragic disruption. There is a fall from grace and a harsh new reality pertains.

This concept of the fall of humankind is currently less centre stage than would have been the case in a medieval mystery play. However, it is an incontrovertible metaphor of the condition in which humanity finds itself. Life as experienced is less than perfect. Environmental harmony is difficult to maintain. Relationships are seriously compromised. These disruptions are the consequences of the central action in Genesis 3. The painful corollary is depicted in all its facets as ruptured relationship. Adam blames Eve. Eve blames the serpent. (The serpent probably blames God, but we don't get to overhear that bit.) The outcome is tragic, clear and sadly totally recognisable. Perfect harmony is no longer a given. Everything and everyone is out of joint. This is the shared experience of the humanity that the book of Genesis seeks to address. This is a recognisable description of life as we now experience it. Perfect start, interrupted, disrupted and lost, leads to struggling existence and the common bleak lot of humanity. So now where?

Relational rescue

'The whole core of biblical history is the story of the calling of a visible community to be God's own people.'[12] Lesslie Newbiggin was one of the most influential missionary thinkers of the 20th century. *The Household of God* was the title of his published Kerr Lectures from 1953, and this quote from his introduction underpinned all that followed. Reading the biblical texts from a missional perspective, Newbiggin tells us that human history is the continuing story of rescuing that ruptured relationship. God's central purpose is to call together a people for himself. The irrevocably relational God will not give up on his avowed intention to be in relationship with his people. A relational God creates relational human beings to live relational lives as part of a relational story. God will do whatever is necessary to overcome any threat to that ultimate outcome.

Abraham and the metaphor of friendship

'But you, Israel, my servant, Jacob, whom I have chosen, you descendants of Abraham my friend' (Isaiah 41:8). God makes friends. Not only does he desire friendship in a generic kind of way with all of humanity, but God invests in a specific relationship. We understand well that God's dealings with the nation of Israel are a kind of model for his purpose for the whole human race. We should not overlook, however, the significance of his dealings with Abraham in particular as the heart of, and metaphor concerning, that bigger picture. This friendship is significant; it will tell us much. Piecing together the biblical references to God and Abraham allows us to draw some serious conclusions about the relational heart of God and his aspirations for wider humankind.

God makes friends with Abraham. God calls on Abraham (Genesis 12:1) and Abraham calls on God (Genesis 12:8). The friendship then matures into the model relationship that becomes a defining metaphor for the life of faith in the Christian believer. Romans 4:16 has it that '[Abraham] is the father of us all'. Both the prophet Isaiah and the writer to the Hebrews (11:8–19) refer back to this friendship and how it stands as a model of the life of faith.

Walter Brueggemann, in his commentary on Genesis,[13] sees in this exchange a depiction of the profound transformation brought about by the life of faith. Abraham's great adventure is primarily a risk-taking engagement with God. God's invitation to Abraham is cast not so much as an injunction to believe certain doctrines, perform certain rituals or even embrace particular ethics. It is a thoroughly relational invitation. Abraham is invited to a journey. 'By faith Abraham, when called to go to a place he would later receive as his inheritance, obeyed and went, even though he did not know where he was going' (Hebrews 11:8). It sounds a lot like the 'Come, follow me' (Mark 1:17), which, in time, we will hear from Jesus. There are no fishing nets to be abandoned for Abraham, but instead a land, a heritage, a patrimony and a way of life to be relinquished in favour of an uncertain future.

Why would he do it? Why would they? Why would anyone? Only out of a risk-taking trust, an all-or-nothing gamble based on genuine affection and true friendship. God is relational, and he plays that card with a flourish. The God of Abraham is a friend-making God. The story of the Old Testament is the story of God's friendship with Abraham and his family. So now to the New Testament.

Jesus and the relational gospel

Weary workmen, reeking of sweat and fish, knotting frayed cord with calloused hands, respond with alacrity to a ridiculously risky invitation from a wandering rabbi. However you recall the scene, from Sunday school, Bible illustration or sermon, the gospel adventure starts out in relational encounter. If, as most agree, Mark was the first written Gospel, then the story kicks off not with the subsequently added birth narratives, nor even with the profound later theological articulations about the person of Jesus or what he accomplished, but rather with a massively relational personal invitation to specific individuals to get up and join in.

If God is as profoundly relational as we have been claiming, then this introduction to the gospel will come as no surprise. What may make a deeper impact on us is the realisation that both message and method are equally relational. Jesus is inviting a disparate group of followers into a profound new set of relationships, with God, with each other and with the wider world. This is the message. This is the method.

The relationship starts with 'Come, follow me'. To be absolutely accurate, the invitation is preceded with an announcement: 'The time has come. The kingdom of God has come near' (Mark 1:15). In the light of that disclosure, Jesus says, 'Come and follow me.' G.E. Ladd, in his book *A Theology of the New Testament*, describes what he calls the classic view of the kingdom as 'the Fatherhood of God and the brotherhood of man'.[14] But he goes further. Ladd then describes how the coming of Jesus actually instigates that kingdom and initiates the new relationships that are possible within it.

This is the new age. The gospel message, on the lips of Jesus, is an invitation to join in this new kingdom. A new set of life-changing relationships have become possible. This is the content of Jesus' message. How does he go about communicating that message? He does it by instigating a set of profoundly life-changing relationships. The gospel method *is* the gospel message. The message *is* the method. It couldn't be more relational if it tried.

Beyond the synoptics

It can be rightly argued that the language of God's kingdom is a feature of the synoptic Gospels: Mark, Luke and Matthew. The fourth Gospel, ascribed to John, prefers the language of life, and life to the full (John 10:10). Whichever way you look at it, it is every bit as relational, possibly more so: 'Love one another... By this everyone will know that you are my disciples' (John 13:34–35). Most unequivocally, in the upper-room discourse (John 14—16) Jesus specifically says, 'I no longer call you servants, because a servant does not know his master's business. Instead, I have called you friends, for everything that I learned from my Father I have made known to you' (John 15:15). The message is a reframed relationship with God; the method is reframed relationship with Jesus.

Here in the fourth Gospel lies the promise that accompaniment will continue: 'It is for your good that I am going away,' says Jesus, somewhat counter-intuitively (John 16:7). Why? Because that will presage the sending of another accompanier. The Holy Spirit (whose work will become clearer in the writings of Luke, as he takes the story beyond the ascension and Pentecost, and into the mission of the primitive church) is specifically promised as a further companion. God promises an accompanying presence, who will be experienced at least in part in the down-to-earth engagements that Christian believers have with one another.

At its best, the accompaniment that we offer one another will be a partial outworking of God's promise that he 'will never leave you nor forsake you' (Deuteronomy 31:6; see also Hebrews 13:5). In chapter 5, 'Jesus and relational discipling', we will look in more detail at the particular style of accompaniment practised by Jesus in relation to his friends.

Paul and relational mission

Beyond the cross and resurrection, after the epoch-defining events that constitute the foundational proclamation of God's activity in Jesus, beyond the initiating drama of Pentecost, Christian mission continues to be primarily relational. The story is still one of restored relationship. The message remains God's invitation to friendship. The gospel imperative continues consistently as a call to join in.

'God was reconciling the world to himself in Christ, not counting men's sins against them. And he has committed to us the message of reconciliation' (2 Corinthians 5:19). This stands as an excellent summary of Paul's first-century mission. The announcement at the heart of the gospel is Jesus' birth, death, resurrection and sending of the Holy Spirit. The purpose behind, and consequence of, those defining actions is the restoration of broken friendship. The God who walked with Adam and Eve, the God who called Abraham his friend, is the God who in Jesus takes responsibility for putting it all right and relentlessly pursues his original intention. The relational God has never wanted anything other than friendship, and in Jesus he has done all that is needful to put the story back on track. Christian mission is now shaped by the retelling of that story, and the reissuing of that invitation.

John and relational mission

The clearest definition of relational Christian mission is found in the letters of John. 1 John 1:3 says, 'We proclaim to you what we have seen and heard, so that you also may have fellowship with us. And our fellowship is with the Father and with his Son, Jesus Christ.' It really couldn't be much clearer. Gospel proclamation concerns the activity of God in Jesus, witnessed first-hand by the apostles. So far, so obvious. It is from that little phrase 'so that' that the punchline is delivered.

'We proclaim the gospel *so that* you can join in with us. We who proclaim are those who have already responded to the invitation to friendship with God and each other. Our task is to continue the story of friend-making. You join us as our new friend. Together we become those who invite yet others to join us in our friendship with God in Jesus, and with each other. New friends make new friends.'

That is Christian mission. That is the continuation of the story of a relational God who refuses to be deflected from the original purpose in the original story.

Revelation and beyond

The canon of Christian scriptures concludes with the book of Revelation: 'God... will dwell with them. They will be his people, and God himself will be with them and be their God' (21:3).

This is what it has always been about. Happily, on this occasion, the answers can be found at the back of the book. He will be their God; they will be his people. The apocalypse concludes with an insight into the ultimate goal of the entire story. And it is relational. This was how it started in the garden; this is how it ends in the new city. The friend-making God has accompanied his people on a journey of exploration that does not find its ultimate fulfilment until he is with them, they are with him and the accompanying relationship is complete.

The big relational picture

What has been explored here, in this chapter, is an examination of major biblical themes which, taken both individually and together, demonstrate conclusively that high-quality, functional relationships are at the heart of a Christian understanding of the world, precisely because they lie at the heart of a Christian understanding of God himself. It is who he is, who we are and what we are for. Relational accompaniment is an outworking of the nature of God. Accompaniment is so much more than a recent discovery, a smart idea or a useful strategy. We are talking about a medium that is itself the message. God is relational.

Your personal reflection

- How did you first become aware of the personal friendship of God?
- What human relationships formed part of that story?
- What for you has been the controlling metaphor of your journey with God to this point?

3

Relational human beings

The human shape

I've just come off the phone to one of the four big UK energy suppliers. After many previous unproductive, tedious calls, I'm close to blowing up with frustration. I tell the story one more time (the details don't matter here). Yet again, I give my own contact information. 'Oh!' the customer service operative replies. 'You weren't the vicar in Washington, were you? My husband became a Christian in your church. How lovely to talk to you.' A classically boring, routine, mind-numbing piece of business is totally transformed into a meaningful moment of human connection. We have contact. Two people, going about their tasks in a seemingly impersonal world, find a connection and the day is suddenly different.

Healthy, stimulating, non-entangled, non-conflicting adult-to-adult relationships lie at the heart of our growth and development as human beings. To return, briefly, to the garden of Eden: there we discovered as a foundational aspect of Christian theology that it was understood to be 'not good' for mankind to be alone. Earlier in the story, and possibly as an earlier strand of the tradition, we read, 'Be fruitful and increase in number; fill the earth and subdue it' (Genesis 1:28). This suggests a measure of relationship to, and responsibility for, the environment in which we find ourselves. Beyond that, it introduces flourishing as an intentional mark of purposeful human living. Human beings have a demanding but satisfying vocation to live and to live well.

We can measure the flourishing of our lives by the quality of our friendships. We express ourselves, reveal ourselves and ultimately discover ourselves only in relation to other people. Both theology and psychology lead us to this secure conclusion.

Swiss doctor Paul Tournier wrote in *The Meaning of Persons*: 'The person, whatever it be, can only be manifested by expressing itself.'[15] Theologian and philosopher Martin Buber, in *I and Thou*, suggested a definition of the individual that is entirely shaped by relationship: 'all real living is meeting'.[16]

Dan Siegel, professor of psychiatry at UCLA, has developed a discipline which he calls 'interpersonal neurobiology'.[17] At its centre is an understanding that the human brain quite literally takes its shape in relation to others. He argues that the neural pathways (internal wiring of the brain) in and for relating connect up prior to the awakening of our own conscious self-awareness. We respond to other people *before* we are actually conscious of ourselves as selves. On that reading, not only are we physically constructed for relationship, but relationship actually defines us and shapes us. We are physiologically made for one another.

Psychological development

Much research has been conducted to demonstrate the tragic consequences of the deprivation of contact with others. Henry Harlow's famous, but sadly disturbing, experiments in the 1950s showed that rhesus monkeys deprived of early contact with their mothers very quickly became anxious, nervous and depressed. This controversial work nevertheless provided the bedrock of researched data concerning the need for affirmation, feedback and stimulus, in order for the individual to develop.

We start out in need of others in order to become truly ourselves. Look at it this way: from conception to birth, we are totally at one with our environment and undifferentiated from the physical context in which we live. The womb is our world and our world is the womb.

From the moment that we emerge, however, kicking and screaming, we are pitched into a journey towards what C.G. Jung called 'individuation'. By this he meant our life's work of discovering who we are, how we are and ultimately why we are. This Jung declared to be the human story.

As we grow up through childhood we progress, step by step, into less dependent, more mature patterns of self-awareness and interaction with others. From the total dependence of infancy, we travel through a growing negotiation with a world in which we are not the centre. Here, personality takes shape, character begins to form and interdependence is explored until we come to stand on the verge of mature adult selves.

Most parents know to their cost the traumatic effect of the teenage years during which the adult persona emerges. This above all is a time of transition. We oscillate between the dependence of children and the maturity of adults. Parenting requires skilful navigation between the nurture that is needed and leaving space for an experiential autonomy to blossom. (You probably can't win either way.) The child will grow, for good or ill, and eventually the adult persona will be formed. Eventually, a measure of maturity will be reached and the adult stands in a relationship of interdependence with the world around.

Christian theology starts from the same understanding of persons. We are unique individuals, with a pressing need for friendship with one another and God. Building on that foundational theology, physiology and psychology, we can venture to suggest that one of the greatest gifts that we can give to another human being is to treat them as a friend. There comes a time when our greatest need is to be engaged with as a grown-up. People's healthy development depends upon others forming with them an adult-to-adult relationship. To do that, as those potential friends, we will need to be well-defined mature adults ourselves.

Insights from transactional analysis

In 1964, the book *Games People Play* was published in the USA by the Canadian psychiatrist Eric Berne.[18] This book, possibly more than any other, brought the hitherto esoteric world of psychology into the public marketplace. Berne was part of that generation of psychiatrists profoundly influenced at the outset by the theories of Sigmund Freud. Like others, in the light of pragmatic experience, he eventually moved away from his Freudian roots and began to piece together a more nuanced but accessible theory of human personality and behaviour. With the eventual publication of *Games People Play*, Berne presented a concept and a language that helped to describe human relationships in clear and simple terms. The fact that this book is still in print 50 years later, and that its central thesis, designated as transactional analysis, is still being quoted (often as a foundation to other, more developed theories), says much about the wisdom contained therein.

Here, in a nutshell, is Berne's central thesis. Every human being starts out life as a dependent infant. Berne describes how all our post-birth experiences of interpersonal relationships are conducted in a context of need and vulnerability. We learn at the outset to see ourselves as weaker in relation to stronger others. The awakening, self-aware individual learns from the beginning to look up to and to depend upon another. In some sad cases, we learn to fear the bigger, more dominant other. Either way, Berne characterises this as child-to-parent relating, and the first relational pattern is formed.

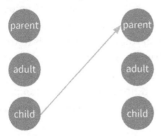

Diagram 1: Child-to-parent relating

As life progresses, the hallmarks of this relational dynamic are continually re-encountered. The chances are that we will meet it again at school in the guise of pupil-to-teacher. We will come across it once more as a pecking order is established in the emerging hierarchy of our peer relationships. At their worst, this becomes bullying and dominance. Later, it crops up as the employee-to-boss relationship. According to Berne's theory, we can expect to relive this dynamic again and again in further subservient-to-dominant contexts throughout later life. Once that pattern of relating becomes embedded, it is described by Berne as an 'ego state'. It becomes deeply rooted in our psyche. Conversational or contextual triggers will then fire up that way of relating subsequently throughout our life. Whenever we find ourselves in relationships of unequal power, we can expect to re-experience this response, whether or not it is appropriate to the situation. David Nobbs in the 1970s novels about Reginald Perrin (later a massively successful TV series) played on this very concept. Reggie's boss C.J. occupied a big chair, behind a large desk, in an imposing office. Whenever he was summoned, Reggie was depicted as small, even shrinking, in the presence of this managerial aggression. This was a classic depiction of damaged child-to-parent relating.

Berne suggests that there is an equally unhelpful alternative outcome. When the now-grown child finally finds herself in a strong or potentially dominant position, then she replays the learned responses from her own previously damaged encounters. Now that she is the dominant one, she adopts the learned patterns and ego state of the controlling parent. The child becomes the parent, the inferior becomes the superior, the dominated becomes the dominator. 'Hurt people hurt people' runs the old adage, constantly reaffirmed from experience by those engaged in the caring professions. Berne describes this as damaged 'parent ego state'. He suggests that it is a replaying of the recorded inner script laid down by those earlier unhappy memories. Previously experienced dominating parental voices provide a pattern for the domination of others. This Berne describes as parent-to-child relating.

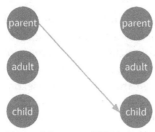

Diagram 2: Parent-to-child relating

Of course, there is a much happier scenario. In the best cases, our more powerful superiors handle their roles with great grace and sensitivity. In that case, we can be nurtured towards maturity and well prepared for healthier later encounters. When we have been cared for in our vulnerability, respected in our weakness and nurtured in our time of dependency, then we can transition positively and gently towards our own independence (or better still interdependence) when the time comes. By being treated as adults, by adults, we can indeed become happily functioning adults ourselves. In such cases, a healthy 'adult ego state' develops. Parents can be nurturing, teachers can be empowering, bosses can be releasing. The goal of all this, in Berne's analysis, is to be found in genuinely autonomous and respectful adult-to-adult relating.

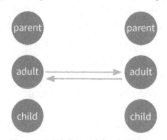

Diagram 3: Adult-to-adult relating

There will be future situations where parenting dynamics are properly called for. There will even be occasions when childlike behaviour is both appropriate and indeed fun. Not all child-to-parent relating is damaged. Not all parent-to-child dealings are unhelpful.

There comes a time, however, when overwhelmingly the need is for individuals to grow into the ability to engage other emerging adults in mutually helpful relationships. At its best, that is what adult-to-adult friendship offers. Hence the suggestion that it is very much more than simply an enjoyable way to conduct ourselves in relation to others. It is vital to our well-being and theirs. It is a gift of great price. It is the central dynamic of accompaniment.

A story from the ward

M. David Enoch, head of clinical psychiatry at Liverpool Hospital and author of *Healing the Hurt Mind*,[19] tells the following true story. An eminent collection of medical professionals was gathered around the hospital bed of a young boy who had very recently made a remarkable and unexpected recovery from severe mental and emotional illness. They were seeking to establish the prime cause of this much welcomed, but unanticipated, outcome. Each was secretly hoping to establish that it had been their particular contribution that had proved decisive. In response to gentle conversational probing, the child indicated without hesitation that it was his new friend who had made all the difference. Each member of the team continued to harbour the aspiration that this was indeed them. 'And just who is your friend who has helped you so much?' the boy was asked. 'Why, him, of course,' he replied, indicating the hospital cleaner.

At great risk, this seems to be the nature of the friendship that God offers to Abraham, Jesus offers to his disciples and we are invited to offer each other. This is the foundational premise of the accompaniment relationship. This is the psychological insight that we will add to our relational theological foundation. Both Accompanier and Accompanied are adults in a mature relationship of mutual respect. There may be occasional elements of parental nurturing, but never dominance. There may be occasional elements of childlike playfulness, but never dependence. Accompanied and Accompanier are equals. Transactional analysis gives us a theoretical psychological base, to add to our biblical theological foundation, from which to interpret our responsibility to each other.

Learning lessons from life

In 1995, I responded to a wave of intrigued fascination that was sweeping the UK Christian constituency. Like very many others, I made the journey to Toronto, to the Airport Christian Fellowship. There had been reports of an unprecedented outpouring of the Holy Spirit. Some people were massively sceptical. Others were convinced this was a major work of God. Most, like me, were simply fascinated and happy to visit with an open mind. The events of those days are well documented, by one of the leaders involved, in Guy Chevreau's *Catch the Fire*.[20] What I can say, without hesitation or fear of contradiction, is that one of the most affecting components of the entire experience was the spontaneous warmth and open friendliness between total strangers. Fellow visitors would greet each other, converse, engage and otherwise relate in hotel lobbies, on buses, in queues, indeed wherever human being came upon fellow human being in a totally delightful and unprecedented way. Quite remarkable.

And now for something completely different. Or is it? Seventeen years later, I was unexpectedly struck by reports that I was hearing from family, friends, neighbours and colleagues as a result of their visits to the London 2012 Olympics. 'We've never experienced anything like it,' they said. Strangers were spontaneously talking with one another. People were being greeted on the streets. Previously unprecedented engagements with fellow passengers were taking place on public transport. It sounded to me a lot like Toronto. Nobody I heard was suggesting that it was an outpouring of the Holy Spirit. But why not? If we are indeed relational human beings, literally shaped for interaction with each other, then surely any positive engagement with one another will carry intimations of God's purpose and our ultimate vocation. Perhaps we need to learn how to see and describe these encounters differently.

The word on the street

The need for good-quality, affirming relationships is not confined to adherents of the Christian faith. If indeed God's is the life behind all life, the shape behind all shape, the purpose behind all purpose, then little wonder that relationship matters in a world that we are convinced takes its shape from God.

The School of Life

Chapter 2 of Alain de Botton's book *Religion for Atheists*[21] is entitled 'Community', and the first subheading is 'Meeting strangers'. The main thesis of the book is well summed up by the title! De Botton is intrigued by the contribution to society of faith communities, but unpersuaded by their competing doctrines. He has clearly tapped into something of significance. His School of Life was received with much acclaim in 2008. This was modelled on much of what he had come to see and appreciate in a faith context, but without the dogmatic component. The basic premise was that people needed a context in which to meet and engage with one another. He could see that faith communities provide that, but what about those who long for the connection, but simply don't buy into the accompanying doctrines? There was a gap in the market for (mostly) young adults in need of the space to explore meaning and the capacity to connect. The book reached the *New York Times* bestseller list. The School of Life charges from £45 for a single session to £700 for a full week. It has 1.7 million subscribers to its YouTube channel. Somebody has clearly recognised the need for human beings to connect in a meaningful way.

Sunday Assembly

In 2013, the first Sunday Assembly event was held in Islington. According to their website, this organisation now hosts around 70 such gatherings in eight different countries. Although not overtly associated with de Botton's movement, the idea looks remarkably similar. The driving issue still seems to be 'how can we facilitate good-quality human interaction without buying into the religious dogma that is usually part of the deal?'

Both of these initiatives, School of Life and Sunday Assembly, have tapped into an understanding of relationally shaped humanity of which the Christian church can ill afford to lose sight. If Irenaeus was at all right in his dictum that 'the glory of God is [hu]mankind fully alive', then an essential part of our self-understanding consists in our vocation to contribute to one another's well-being in the shape of great adult-to-adult relationships.

Professional research into the human condition

The Centre for Economic Policy Research (CEPR) brings together a network of researchers from universities across Europe. In December 2016, they presented their latest findings at a conference organised by the Organisation for Economic Cooperation and Development (OECD) and hosted by the London School of Economics (LSE). This work is now available in book form, *The Origins of Happiness*.[22] The conference was opened by Lord Gus O'Donnell, former UK government Cabinet Secretary. (I think we have established that this was a serious piece of work conducted by credible academics and therefore worth taking note of.) The central finding of this major investigation was that the mental health of individuals was the single greatest influence on levels of contentment among the population. Emotional well-being has a more profound impact than income, employment, physical health or education. The purpose of the conference was to make the case that, from a policy point of view, investment in people's well-being was within the grasp of government. It is possible to make a difference, and addressing the emotional and relational needs of people is the single best way to go about it.

Lesson learned?

They are singing our song. Psychologists and pragmatists, academics and entrepreneurs are swelling the chorus. Human beings crave great relationships. Undergirding our concept of accompaniment is a foundational theological conviction concerning the relational nature of God. Human life reflects that nature, and we are not the only ones saying so. In addition to our deeply held spiritual convictions, psychology and recent research into human nature reveal a deep and lasting need for good, positive, health-giving relationships. We are standing on solid ground, and marking it out as our territory.

From relational God and relational human beings, we will move in the next chapter to consider the absolute necessity of relational church.

Your personal reflection

Pause for a moment first.

- When have you most been aware of being in a positive, life-enhancing adult-to-adult relationship?
- What did and does that feel like for you?
- How can you more intentionally build that into your own dealings with others?
- To which specific relationships can you make the most positive contribution?

4

Relational church

A lesson from the Alpha Course

I am a very big fan of the Alpha Course. As chance would have it, I wrote the advertising copy for the initial publicity campaign that went around the world in several different translations: 'An opportunity to explore the meaning of life – starting soon at a church near you.' Both Michael Moynagh[23] and the *Mission-Shaped Church* report (2004)[24] refer to the story of HARVEST New Anglican Church that we started in 1998, out of the work that had been done through Alpha. We quickly learned that its effectiveness lay not so much in the content of the course but in the relationships that it facilitated. Week after week, in course after course, participants would say something like, 'I still have no idea what you're on about, but I have to keep coming because of the friends I've made here.'

Working as an Alpha advisor and facilitator for churches around Kent, I was saddened, but not surprised, repeatedly to find congregations that had run highly effective Alpha courses, only to lose touch with their new contacts once the course was completed. The reason was almost always the same. The transition from highly relational conversation-based evenings into sadly impersonal Sunday congregational events just wasn't happening. We were rediscovering what we should always have known about the priority of facilitating good healthy relationships: people are massively more interested in meeting other people than in attending an impersonal event.

Theology goes to church

It should have come as no surprise. Back in 1978, the eminent German theologian Jürgen Moltmann produced a little book entitled *The Open Church*.[25] It was a light-touch re-presentation of some of the material found in his much weightier and highly influential *The Church in the Power of the Spirit*, published the previous year.[26] Fascinatingly, there is a chapter in Moltmann's 2015 book *The Living God and Fullness of Life* entitled 'Freedom experienced in open friendship' that reads remarkably like the same text![27] But then, if you have lighted upon an essential truth, why wouldn't you repeat it as often as you could? If it's worth saying once…

Moltmann talks of a passion for living, so often missing from his experience of formal church. He describes what he calls the 'Messianic lifestyle' to which the church is invited. He believes passionately (enough to be saying the same thing for 40 years) that this quality of life needs to be expressed in mutual acceptance. This, in turn, facilitates the risk-taking necessary to experience change and growth. 'When others look at us in a friendly way, we feel alive and vital'; 'We stand on firm ground whenever we accept, recognise and confirm each other.'[28] This is sounding like the relational dynamic described in the first letter of John ('that you also may have fellowship with us. And our fellowship is with the Father,' 1 John 1:3) to which Christian mission always aspires.

As Moltmann unfolds his central thesis, it strongly echoes the insights that we have discovered in Eric Berne's theory of adult-to-adult relationship:

> In the fellowship of Jesus, the disciples become friends of God. In the fellowship of Jesus, they no longer experience God as Lord, nor only as Father; rather they experience him in his innermost nature as friend. For this reason, open friendship becomes the bond in their fellowship with one another, and it is their vocation in a society still dominated by masters and

servants, fathers and children, teachers and pupils, superiors and subordinates.[29]

Our definition of accompaniment is therefore deeply rooted in the concept of relational church. A relational God calls relational human beings together into the fellowship of relational church. Bishop Lesslie Newbiggin, in his Kerr Lectures, later published as *The Household of God*, quoted earlier, makes the point that church is more than a repository of doctrines and practices. The church has a story to tell, of course; there is a gospel to proclaim. But behind, underneath, above and around that, it is the vocation of the church to *be* something. Probably the most often-quoted aphorism from Lesslie Newbiggin is the insight that 'the only hermeneutic of the gospel is a community that lives by it'. The authenticity of our living and the relationships that undergird our communal life are our most powerful and effective means of communication. If the church desires more faithfulness to its calling, it needs to look with greater honesty, not at its management style or its preaching technique, but at the quality of life at its heart.

Insights from Fresh Expressions

This is a new day for the church. (Isn't it always? Perhaps this is newer than most.) Things are changing fast – not fast enough for some, to be sure, but quite dramatically on the longer view. Within a lifetime, many of our mainline denominations have embraced change that renders Sunday gatherings unrecognisable from the remembered events of childhood. Congregations in their 'Sunday best' would worship with formats that had not changed for generations. They would sing music that mostly went back a hundred years or more. The involvement of children was largely unheard of. It was at least in part the failure of this culture to connect with upcoming generations that provided the impetus to explore new forms of church. We are still very much in the throes of this reimagining and reshaping process. It is far from complete. We do now have a body of literature, studies and documentation to help make sense of the movement.

Quality relationships: inside and out

Two pieces of research in particular are relevant to our exploration of the centrality of relationship to the church's calling, and to the psychological well-being of the people within. *Natural Church Development* (NCD) by Christian Schwarz was first published in the UK by the British Church Growth Association in 1996.[30] I am mildly qualified to reflect on this work because I (and the church I was leading at the time) was part of the initial research project on which the work was based. This project was unusual and differed from much of what was then current in Church Growth circles because of its use of hard data rather than anecdote. Here was an attempt to shed light on what was actually happening. Why were some churches growing when others clearly were not? Were there truths to be found that could provide a solid basis for future planning and strategy?

Indeed, there were. Schwarz's research, conducted from the German Institute for Church Development, identified eight 'quality characteristics' that were determinant for the flourishing of church life. These marks, so the research demonstrated, would be observably present in healthy church life and largely absent in the opposite. Over the years, this qualitative approach has been honed and nuanced. The data has been added to by further research and the insights worked out in practice in countless other church communities. (In fact, they record having collated more than four million survey responses in over 70,000 different churches worldwide.) At its heart, they identify loving relationships as being among the most essential factors for health and growth.

Steve Aisthorpe quotes the work of NCD in his 2016 book *The Invisible Church*.[31] Aisthorpe's book is answering quite a different question. It is also very well researched. It presents, in readable form, the work conducted for his doctoral thesis on church decline. In the event, *The Invisible Church* describes a whole generation of people who have not actually turned their collective backs on the content of Christian faith, but rather on the practical expression of it, as found in traditional church structures. Aisthorpe recorded hundreds of interviews with individuals who had concluded, often reluctantly, that church, as currently experienced, was no longer the place to encounter life that expresses the calling of Jesus. Hence the 'invisible church' of the title, a body of people who no longer feel that they belong. There is one rather garbled but unmistakeably passionate quote that is repeated twice in the book, because it encapsulates the heart of the findings:

> I'm really – stopping myself because I can just hear myself what I've said, that the love – is because there isn't love. It's actually because there isn't that people are sitting outside the church. Do you know, I actually realised that is it. I'm feeling it in my heart, because I'm saying it out loud. I hadn't actually thought it as conclusively as that. There is not the love. In the church if the love of Christ is not coming through from top to bottom… The church has got to learn to love again – that is it, that – is – it![32]

A chance to start again: the HARVEST story

What would church look like if we had the opportunity to begin over again? By 1998, I had been in parish ministry for 20 years. I had worked in four different churches in various parts of the country. Three of them were large to start with, and one grew to be that way. (Michael Parkinson, in a radio interview, had suggested that if the Church of England paid by results then I might have retired on the spot.) For some peculiar reason, I was more content in the small-church setting than the larger one. I was struggling with the William James disclosure quoted earlier:

> I am done with great things and big plans, great institutions and big success. I am for those tiny, invisible loving human forces that work from individual to individual, creeping through the crannies of the world like so many rootlets, or like

the capillary oozing of water, which, if given time, will rend the hardest monuments of pride.

Whatever the reason, discontent with the large-church model, exhaustion from trying to match up to my own and others' expectations, or just a deep human desire for more fulfilling and meaningful relationships, I found myself in the enviable position of literally being able to start again.

One further component in the shaping of 'HARVEST' had stemmed from the emergence of cell-church thinking. Around this time, there had been an influx of information filtering through from the cellular models of church life being pioneered in Singapore and beyond. Here was a model that seemed to take seriously the Natural Church Development insight that quality relationships lay at the heart of flourishing church. This was sometimes still large church, occasionally even mega-church, but structured around a multiplicity of multiplying small groups.

We discovered over time that there was still a strong element of directional leadership required if the cell model were to be pursued rigorously. Like other colleagues in the UK, we decided ultimately not to push it that far.[33] What mattered was the emphasis on the small. Having made a persuasive case to the bishop, particularly along the lines of, 'Isn't it time that someone somewhere was allowed to pioneer something different?', we were given permission to start again. Thus HARVEST New Anglican Church was born.

To our consternation, both bishop and archdeacon were agreed on a number of deeply unsettling corollaries. First, I would have to resign the incumbency of the parish church in order to lead the new plant. It couldn't be done, they said, from the security of a freehold parish clergy post. The risk, including the financial one, would have to be ours. In practice, that meant that we were given twelve months of monetary underpinning, after which we would need to be contributing to diocesan budgets like any other Church of England congregation. The level at which we would be expected to pay in would be a realistic one, but there would be no subsidy. No other parish would be asked or expected to contribute to our survival. 'If this is how you think the Church of England should be able to operate, then prove it.' I am not sure any of the diocesan hierarchy actually put it that way, but that was clearly what was meant!

On top of that, we were not permitted to advertise our presence. Seriously. No posters, no flyers, no notices in shop windows. Not even a notice on the information board of the primary school in which we were to meet, Sunday by Sunday. That was because we were to remain loyally Anglican. That being so, we were inevitably meeting and operating in someone else's parish. (The Church of England, as the established national church, takes responsibility for every home in the land; there is no neutral territory.) We were therefore not to impinge publicly on the work of the parish in which we were located. We could build church only through the relational networks of our initial planting team. Invitations could be word of mouth only. Our bluff had been well and truly called.

At the time, the description 'Fresh Expressions' had not been coined, but we fondly imagine that the HARVEST experience helped to bring it about. Six years later, we were given a small mention in the 2004 *Mission-Shaped Church* report. Unwittingly, we had been part of a movement whose time had come. In the following days, our story featured in several of the publications that were chronicling the emergence of this new movement within UK church life. We seem to have been on to something.

Deeper lessons

One of the most striking features of the early days of HARVEST was the wide diversity of individuals who were welcomed into the network. As relational church (with a cell-church influence), the emphasis was always on the small groups. Sunday-morning gatherings were held each week, but that was not the main focus of church life. The weekly coming together of the small-group network for corporate worship, teaching input and mutual encouragement was a low-key affair. All the emphasis was placed on the relationships within each small group. The core planting team consisted of twelve people, with a wider network of about 50. Over the first five years of its life, the HARVEST network drew in more than 200 individuals who made meaningful connection with those groups.

HARVEST members came from an impressive array of backgrounds. There was a majority from what is now often called the 'de-churched'. These were men and women who had given up on church life in other contexts. Some had been Roman Catholics, others Pentecostal. Some had been Orthodox, others had belonged to the so-called House Church movement. Nearly all had become disenchanted and disengaged from institutions and structures that they felt had limited rather than enhanced their sense of self, their search for meaning and their encounter with God and other people. Most of them came with their particular theological influences still in place, which made life interesting. Fundamentalist creationists would sit with liberal-minded spiritual seekers. Politically active left and right wingers found themselves part of the same family. We had our moments; of course we did. There were fall-outs and confrontations. But, if you were part of HARVEST, then you had committed to the core values of relational engagement above and beyond political and theological differences.

There were some equally marked contrasts in income levels and social background. Drug users and head teachers belonged equally (not that there is necessarily a distinction between the two); successful entrepreneurs and those who had never done a day's work in their life met in a context of mutual acceptance. We felt that this was different. It was what we had longed for. It was tough to maintain, but, despite several cycles of growth and decline, it still continues at the time of writing, nearly 20 years later.

Core lessons for accompaniment

There is a Chinese proverb of the 'teach a person to fish' genre. It goes, 'If you want to prosper for a year, grow grain. If you want to prosper for a decade, grow trees. If you want to prosper for a lifetime, grow people.' The HARVEST experience was one of growing people. Quite often that resulted in loss for the church but gain for the wider community. The cell-church theory had envisaged growing leaders for new cell groups from within the group itself. It promised a model of exponential continuous growth. In practice, what we discovered was that, by growing people, we had opened up a whole new vista of possibilities for them, and not only within the confines of church life.

On several occasions, key individuals who had grown in ability, maturity and aspiration found themselves faced with unexpected and exciting prospects. Promotion at work was quite regular. Sometimes our people would be headhunted for a demanding new role, either at work or in the local community. Either way, there would be a significant dilemma. Do we take the job opportunity, the community role or more responsibility in church life? As a principle, we established early on that it was better to give than to receive. We became a 'sending church' and our mission field was often local community life.

One feature of HARVEST Sunday gatherings was the occasional series of talks given by members of the small groups about their workday responsibilities. They would tell us what it meant for them to follow Jesus into the wider world of school, office, hospital, local authority or business. We could count in hundreds the employees for whom our members had responsibility, and in millions the budgets they controlled. We were very definitely helping to grow people.

The fundamental core value at work in HARVEST was the relational accompaniment of existing and potential leaders. My prime task as senior minister was the development of the leadership team. Their prime task was the accompanying development of the group leaders in their care. Those leaders in turn carried the responsibility for developing the group members in their care. It was, and remains, a culture of mutual development.

The cared-for caring for others

One of the most frequently encountered challenges of congregational life is the care of particularly hurting people. Churches quite rightly attract individuals with very great and obvious needs. In practice, what often happens is that a minister will acquire a small caseload of deeply demanding pastoral contacts. The number will usually be determined by the caring capacity of the particular minister. The same is often true for the congregation as a whole. A small number of particularly hurting people will be drawn to the offer of sympathy, support and pastoral care. Those who receive it stay, and thus the congregation settles at a level determined by its available resources of time, empathy and patience.

The HARVEST model was to treat every single individual as having the capacity to care for, help support and ultimately develop other people. That way, care was readily available, but always on the understanding that you in your turn would be part of a giving as well as a receiving pattern. Some, understandably, felt that their needs could be better met elsewhere. Others, though, discovered a whole new vocation as a giver of care and attention. We all continue to need input from others throughout our lives. A context that allows for that adult-to-adult relating as one component of an economy of mutual accompaniment was, for us, a breakthrough.

Love one another

The research cited above by Christian Schwarz and Steve Aisthorpe, the ecclesiology articulated by Jürgen Moltmann and the anecdotal evidence of the HARVEST story all point convincingly in the same direction. Church should always be about the quality of relationship demonstrated and experienced within and then carried beyond. Our theological exploration into the relational nature of God should lead us to expect nothing different. The overview of human nature, articulated from both biblical theology and contemporary psychology, leads us in this very same pathway. The deepest need of human beings is to be accompanied. We find ourselves to be formed in the image of a relational God. We recognise our vocation to live relationally with one another, for the better development of each. We conclude that the calling of the church is to be the prime community in which these qualities are experienced and lived out. Mission, for us, is the challenge to live this out in the context of real life as we know it.

Next, it will be time to look more deeply at the life and ministry of Jesus. What can we discover of the same principles at work? Before that, another pause for personal reflection.

Your personal reflection

- When have you experienced relational church at its best?
- Being as honest as you are able, what aspiration do you bring to your dealings with others?
- What, for you, are the signifiers of healthy relationships in a church family?
- How much of that have you been able to receive? Or to give?

5

Jesus and relational discipling

It's now time to turn our attention towards Jesus. If relational accompaniment is anything like as significant as we are making it out to be, then we should expect to find it practised, modelled and commended in the life and ministry of Jesus. We would find it not simply referenced in passing, not just making an appearance in the occasional encounter, not cropping up from time to time, but unmistakably woven through the entire narrative, shaping and driving the story forward. Is that the case?

Jesus-shaped accompaniment

To start, this time, at the end. The disciples have gathered on a hillside, familiar territory for momentous disclosure of lasting significance. Is this a literal description or a literary device? Quite probably it is both. On a hillside, Jesus imparts the beatitudes. On a hillside, Jesus is transfigured. On a hillside, he is crucified. Now, on a hillside, he meets for one final encounter with his closest followers, associates and indeed friends. 'Go into all the world. Go to every ethnic group. Teach. Baptise. Above all, and as a summary of all else, make disciples' (Matthew 28:19, loosely but faithfully translated). Embedded in the following verse is the phrase 'teaching them to obey everything I have commanded you'. It was a long-established rabbinic practice to prepare pupils for the continuation of the teacher's ministry. The principle at the heart of any form of apprenticeship is the handing on of skill from one generation to the next. That was already established practice in Jesus' day, both in practical skills, such as the woodworking, implement making, house-building employment of Jesus' family home in Nazareth, and in the handing on of spiritual tradition. Often quoted is the saying, usually attributed to Rabbi Eliezer, that 'a good pupil is like a limed cistern that does not lose a drop'. Receive it, take it on board, and pass it on.

Continuing to work backwards through the Gospel story, what will we discover to be the shape and content of the material that the disciples have been trained to continue? What will they have imbibed so thoroughly by the time of this final hilltop encounter that it will become second nature to live it out and pass it on? What is the unique content of the life-shaping encounter that this particular group have experienced? Will it be as relational as we now expect?

To the upper room

Back in the upper room of John 13—17, we find the setting for the longest consistent account of Jesus' interaction with his followers at one specific moment in time. Any consideration of the text will lead us to conclude that this material is absolutely and overwhelmingly relational. Here, in the last and fullest account of conversation between Jesus and his followers, there is surprisingly very little dogmatic material. It would be hard to construct creedal statements of belief from these chapters, although some have tried. Instead of instruction, these words are consistently focused on the present and continuing relationship between Jesus and his disciples, between Jesus and his heavenly Father, between disciples and the world, between disciple and disciple – not forgetting the relationship between Holy Spirit and disciples, of which more later.

Here, in the upper room, is the context in which we hear Jesus' instruction to love one another. Here they are commanded to wash one another's feet, although not until they have learned how to be on the receiving end of such ministrations themselves. Here they are promised an organic participation in the life of Jesus, illustrated with a powerful image of vine and branches. Here they are called friends for the first time, and not simply rabbinical students. And here they are promised that the accompanying friendship experienced in their walking with Jesus will in fact be continued by another in days to come. (That's the promise of the Holy Spirit and, like the disciples, we are still going to wait a while before seeing its fulfilment.)

Provoking aspiration

Because of what they have seen in Jesus, the disciples want more. Buddhism has a fund of anecdotes about this kind of learning. Stories abound of the amusing dullness of novices and the short shrift that they often received from their patient but gnomic teachers.

A Zen master had for many years been discipling a pupil who had now risen to hold a high office. Despite their vast difference in social status in the outside world, they had remained in master-to-pupil dealings when alone. One day, the high official asked his teacher, 'Master, what is egotism?' Quick as a flash, the master replied, 'What a wretchedly stupid question; how can you be so dull; haven't you learned anything yet?' The senior official bristled visibly, his face flushed and he began to splutter, 'How dare you!' 'That is,' said the master.

The post-Reformation Christian disciple is quite understandably suspicious of showing subservience to any human teacher. That place properly belongs to Jesus, and in the post-Pentecost era to the ministry of the Holy Spirit. However, there is a strand of spiritual theology that says the greatest influence that one human being can have upon another is to awaken a 'thirst for more'. 'A holy minister is an awesome weapon in the hands of God,' said Robert Murray M'Cheyne, an early 19th-century evangelical hero of the faith. 'My people's greatest need is my personal holiness' was the sentence that he reputedly kept as a sign on his desk. This may not be a currently fashionable view of spirituality, or even ministry (M'Cheyne died aged 29 having pushed himself to the limits), but the principle is clear. A more amusing, down-to-earth, version can be found at the movies: 'You make me want to be a better person,' says the wayward Melvin to Carol in the 1997 film *As Good As It Gets*.

Returning to safer ground, 'Deep calls to deep' is how the psalmist puts it (Psalm 42:7). Something profoundly true in the life of one person finds an echo in the life of another. By living with integrity, by demonstrating spiritual maturity in the everyday world, one stirs something in the other. We always thought there was more, and when we brush up against it in a fellow human being, the longing is awakened. 'When I grow up I want to be like…'

'I have called you friends'

Back in the upper room, Jesus has stirred something of this kind of deep but poorly articulated longing in the life of his followers. 'Show us the Father,' says Philip. 'How can we know the way?' asks Thomas. 'Wash my hands and my feet as well,' implores Peter. This provides the context in which Jesus now makes that defining declaration of friendship. This is when the uniqueness of kingdom relationships is revealed, and where Jesus spells out the most significant difference in the new model. We have seen something of the rabbinical style of pupil-to-teacher relating. We notice something similar in the Buddhist dynamic of novice to master. Now, in the context of awakened longing for more, Jesus radically shifts the relationship.

> I no longer call you servants, because a servant does not know his master's business. Instead, I have called you friends, for everything that I learned from my Father I have made known to you.
> JOHN 15:15

What exactly is it that has been made known? Do we, like some first-century Gnostic sect, think there is a secret body of knowledge hidden away somewhere from unworthy prying eyes? No, there is no secret; it just seems like one when we wake up to it for the first time. What has been made known, supremely and above all, is exactly that new relational dynamic of which he now speaks. Relational accompaniment *is* the gospel.

The dynamics of Jesus-shaped accompaniment

It is time now to get back to the more familiar territory of the synoptic Gospel narratives. Now we can ask, 'To what extent is relational accompaniment not just the gospel method but actually the gospel message?' What does Jesus-shaped accompaniment actually look like in its historical context?

The book *A Passionate Life* by Mike Breen and Walt Kallestad[34] has quickly become a classic among those looking for a simple, understandable, transferrable model of Christian living. The 'Lifeshapes' around which the book is built take simple geometric figures and use them to propose memorable schemas for interpreting some of the basic dynamics of discipleship. Among the figures used is what they call the Discipleship Square. This square illustrates the progressive developing journey of the first disciples. The four sides of the square are taken to represent four stages of journeying with Jesus.

Side one is illustrative of a time of high dependency during the initial stages of the story. Jesus has called the disciples to be with him; nets have been left; tax franchises are abandoned; political causes are relinquished; relational engagement has begun. A new relationship with Jesus has been instigated, and, by implication, new relationships with fellow followers entered into. There may be, and probably is, great excitement, high energy, significant expectation. But there is little awareness, not much information, a great deal of uncertainty and no preparation for what lies ahead. At this early juncture, the relationship is very much one of master-to-pupil, called by name indeed, but massively dependent. This could be understood as a time of apprenticeship.

The second side of the square, and representing the next chapter in the story as well as the next stage on the journey, comes when things start to go wrong. This is the point at which the disciples discover that not everything works as smoothly or simply as once hoped. 'Why could we not cast it out?' 'No, Lord, this could never be.' The role of Jesus shifts during this phase from the recognisable master-to-pupil, to one of coach-to-player. (More of this dynamic and its choice of language in chapter 6, 'Relational coaching'.) This is where Jesus provokes reflection. He does not simply offer answers. Not, 'You shouldn't do it this way; do it that way'; rather 'What were you talking about on the road?', or 'Who do people say I am?'

Moving on to the third side of the square, we reach the point in the story where Jesus takes more time to build the relationship. Here, he invests in the disciples and takes them beyond initial enthusiasm and subsequent failure to a stage where competence begins to form. 'You give them something to eat.' Actually, they can't; they have to confer together and come back to Jesus for help. But now they are beginning to take responsibility for their own actions and acknowledge their own limitations.

Finally, and on the fourth, concluding side of the square, they will be entrusted with the future of the mission. They will gather on the hillside and Jesus will commission them. They will be instructed to wait for the next phase of accompaniment when the Holy Spirit will lead them into truth, clothe them with power and be with them to the end of the age. Their formation stage will be complete, but accompaniment will continue. The Holy Spirit will accompany; they will accompany; accompaniment will continue to provide the shape of the story. The relational dynamic is not to be abandoned as if it were an adjunct to an earlier phase. This discipleship square is not simply a building block buried away in the foundations. This is the essential shape of the building itself, integral to the overall design, determinative of the architectural integrity of the relational structure of continuing mission.

And, finally, here comes the Holy Spirit

Like the disciples, we have been waiting some little while, under a promise of more from the Holy Spirit. Back in the upper room, at the same time that Jesus reveals the true nature of his accompanying friendship, he tells them that he is on the verge of departure. It sounds almost tragic. Just as a radical fresh understanding of their relationship dawns, it appears to be over. But that is not the whole story. This is where the promise of the Holy Spirit comes to light. Now is the time for the concept of 'another' to be introduced. Now the promise makes most satisfying sense. 'Another advocate to help you and be with you for ever' (John 14:16). Another friend, another accompanier – the model is secured.

This is the 'journeying with' model of discipleship that is integral to the ministry of Jesus. Jesus invites individuals to a journey with himself, and thereby with other disciples. When he commissions them for the next phase, it is to continue modelling with others what he has modelled with them. Matthew 28:19–20 is then a 'go and make disciples' invitation to an accompanied and accompanying lifestyle. Mission *is* accompaniment. We are talking not just about the best method of pursuing mission ('We'll build supportive relationships with others as a way of getting the job done'), but of the very task itself (building supportive relationships with others *is* the actual work to which we are called). Relational accompaniment is the good news of a relational God who calls relationally shaped humanity into a relational church to pursue a relational mission.

Your personal reflection

Before we move on to a consideration of insights from the world of coaching, take some time to think through what you have just read. Bring your own story, with its unique influences, to the conversation.

- What are your longest-held assumptions about discipleship?
- What does discipleship look like in your own everyday world?
- What models of learning from Jesus, and others, have helped you best?
- How are your views, attitudes or behaviour being challenged, shaped or changed right now?

6

Relational coaching

A tourist's guide to the language of journeying together

Up to now, we have been working with the language of accompaniment, without attempting to differentiate it from its many constituent concepts. The working definition, offered at the outset, ran like this:

Accompaniment is consistent engagement, with individuals or teams, for the greater flourishing of their lives and work. It will include elements of coaching, mentoring and simple friendship. It will reveal its greatest value as each of those elements is combined and transcended.

The principles and practices of accompaniment will be equally applicable at the start, the middle and the end of a journey of faith. They will make a significant contribution to discipling, to supporting ministry and to developing leadership roles. They will inform and enhance coaching, mentoring and indeed simple friendship. They will contribute to our flourishing in all that God has intended for us as friends and colleagues. They will make a difference for the kingdom of God.

Before we turn in this chapter to a detailed model of coaching, it may be worthwhile taking a brief tour around the vocabulary. There is a range of language currently used with reference to the concept of developing others. Where are the similarities? What are the differences? Does it matter which words we use? I suggest there is much overlap, some significant difference and, yes, it does matter because we can be all the richer for unpicking the subtle nuances and working more skilfully with shades of light and dark, highlight and shadow, chiaroscuro and contrast.

If we think of the whole field of relational development as a spectrum, it may look something like this, with the most intentional, directive, instructional aspect at the start and the lightest, non-directional touch at the far end:

Apprenticeship – Mentoring – Coaching – Friendship

Apprenticeship

At the tender age of 15, I abandoned home and school. I had previously absconded from my cathedral boarding school and somehow become deeply embroiled in the world of horse racing. As an apprentice, it was my responsibility to muck out, feed and water, ride out, dress down and take to the races the horses in my care. These animals were worth many thousands of pounds and no one was about to entrust that investment entirely to the foibles of a frail youth. I was told what to do. I was shown how to do it. I was shouted at (picking up a rich and colourful vocabulary of abuse in the process) if I didn't do exactly as I had been told and shown. That was apprenticeship.

Mentoring

Returning briefly to the world of the Old Testament scriptures, the books of Kings provide a familiar example of a mentoring relationship. In 1 Kings 19, the prophet Elijah is given specific instruction to recruit Elisha to become his successor. The biblical tradition does not offer great detail about the nature of the relationship between the two men. What is clear is that, at the close of 1 Kings 19, Elisha is no more than an 'attendant'. By 2 Kings 2, however, Elisha is ready to take on the mantle of his master. Elisha is successor, inheritor and ready to emulate and, in some respects, surpass Elijah. This is what we mean by mentoring and, like apprenticeship, it usually starts with a high degree of dependency. The mentor needs to be a person of previously acquired skill and competence. The mentor has an investment in the future capability of the pupil. This relationship includes components of apprenticeship, but will go some way beyond it.

Coaching

Coaching is the focus of this present chapter. It includes the impartation of skills, as when a football team coach drills the players in particular aspects of positioning, defence and attack. When the chips are down, however, it is the one coached who must deliver. The coach is aiding performance only. As this chapter will show, that will sometimes be through the handing on of personally owned capabilities, but can, on occasion, be delivered to a surprisingly high level by someone without any experience at all of the actual goal to be achieved. Coaching is as much about the individual as it is the task. It will focus on attitude as well as on competences.

Friendship

At the far end of the spectrum, not actually required by any of the preceding concepts, lies friendship. This we have seen to be the original purpose and ultimate goal of the relationship between God and humankind. Christian mission in general, and discipleship in particular, will at best look a lot like friendship. 'Discipling' is capable of including any or all of those earlier concepts. To the extent to which discipling comes closest to apprenticeship and mentoring, however, it will sail closest to the wind of manipulation. Friends can mentor, coach or even apprentice, but it is intentional accompaniment that will offer the greatest overlap.

Accompaniment

Sitting outside the spectrum, drawing on all and enhancing each component, lies accompaniment. As defined here, accompaniment may draw on aspects of apprenticeship, mentoring or coaching, but will more consistently be a much lighter-touch relationship. As unpacked in later chapters, it will be seen to be about consistency. It will be about accountability, not to another but to one's own commitments. It will be concerned with affirmation and encouragement, and will focus on clarity of thought, action and outcome. Accompaniment can offer purposeful, acquirable, transferrable skills to the best of friendships. The accompanier will hold this spectrum in mind and work at developing a new understanding of relationship. By understanding more of accompaniment, we can become better, more life-enhancing friends. We will discover that we can make a positive difference. We can offer a specifically Jesus-shaped, Christianity-honed contribution to a spectrum of developmental concepts. Our ultimate goal is a gospel-informed, kingdom-oriented inspiration to fulfilled living.

Coaching: the GROW model

Now to a more detailed description of one particular component of that spectrum, namely coaching.

This part of the story starts with a former British racing driver. Back in the 1980s, John Whitmore was developing an influential model of coaching for the sporting and business worlds. Sir John does not claim to be the originator, but he is credited with shaping and popularising what is now called the GROW model of coaching. The GROW model gained prominence with the publication of his book *Coaching for Performance* in 1992, which has now sold over half a million copies.[35]

GROW is a simple, four-part, coaching acronym. It is designed to be memorable and easy to understand and use. It has the added bonus of being eminently transferrable. I have seen it in action, taught it over a two-day workshop and then taken it into practice with immediate effect. Myles Downey is the founding director of the London School of Coaching; his book *Effective Coaching* (1999) takes the GROW model as a given.[36] He describes how good coaching practice develops intuitively, but commends GROW as the most effective summary of best practice. In church circles, the interdenominational national Fresh Expressions team regularly runs training events based on this model.

It works like this: G stands for Goal, R for Realities, O for Options and W for Will. Each of these headings summarises one key component of any coaching conversation. Taken together, they provide a framework for all coaching engagements. This is not to be understood as a rigid formula. It would be rare for a coach to stick doggedly to an agenda of four equal constituent parts. Most creative coaching encounters would, however, revolve around and include each one of these elements. The idea, if not the actual language, would normally shape a coaching session. So, how does it work in practice?

Goals

'What do we need to work on today?' is a clear, if understated, approach to initial goal-setting. 'Can we be clear at the outset about just what ground we think would be most helpful to cover?' 'Is there a particular issue or pressure that it would be useful for us to address?' These are good, positive, ways to establish the purpose and desired outcome of a coaching session. It can be surprisingly helpful just to be encouraged to articulate our aspirations. It is easy to assume that we know, intuitively, what it is that we are after. But that simple initial question can work wonders in revealing any fuzziness of thinking and can help to bring into focus our most pressing priorities. Seeking clarity of language leads to clarity of thought, which in turn leads to clarity of outcome, and that is always the goal of the coach. Great accompaniment learns from the coaching model and draws out articulated aspiration.

Starting with the language of goals can, however, sometimes be counterproductive. 'That's great. We do this at work. Really helpful,' says one person at a workshop where I am introducing these principles. 'Oh no. That reminds me of work!' says another. Many areas of life and work are beset with a need to tick boxes. When coaching begins to sound anything like sales targets or the bottom line of a balance sheet, then we can be pretty sure that we are not in a happy place in regard to accompaniment. Understanding the initial 'goal' component of coaching reminds us of the value of clearly articulated outcomes. Holding on to a theologically informed understanding of accompaniment will remind us that the highest value resides with the person and the relationship. Goals imposed on us, as targets by another, are a burden. Goals which are a clarification of our own aspirations are a boon.

Realities

The function of the Realities component in the GROW model of coaching is to elicit the greatest possible honesty about current context. 'So what is specifically preventing you from achieving this desired outcome?' The perceived fog around a swathe of difficult circumstances can be lifted, or at least broken through in patches, by reducing an overwhelming sense of hindrance to its constituent parts. 'Why exactly is that particular factor holding you back?' 'What is the actual nature of the opposition that you fear in that course of action?' Often the simpler question 'Who exactly are "*they*"?' is the most appropriate response to vaguely articulated fears such as, 'They would never let me...' or 'They wouldn't understand if...' Followed up swiftly by, 'What precisely wouldn't they let you do, or don't they understand?'

'It all seems too difficult just now,' said one of my overwhelmed colleagues in a recent coaching session. 'Okay,' I replied, 'let's accept that for now,' and then, after a pause, I asked, 'What specifically is too difficult?'

The coach is not looking to belittle the sense of current defeat, or to minimise the sense of constraint. Rather, the coach's task is to bring the situation into the light and examine it, and the individual's response to it, from all sides. We are where we are. No coaching, and certainly no accompaniment, is worth the name if it tries to pretend otherwise. If the first task of coaching is to clarify goals, it is quickly followed by an honest appraisal of just why we haven't achieved that already. The coach needs to be sufficiently astute to ask the incisive question. She also needs to be sufficiently non-judgemental to allow potentially painful self-awareness to surface. I often find myself using phrases such as 'Let's hold on to that insight for the moment, and then ask…' There can be a false expectation that an accompanier should counter negativity and offer a more positive response. There is also an inkling that a true friend would do the opposite and endorse the bleakness of the situation. ('Oh, I know. Isn't it awful?') Non-directive coaching, of the GROW-model variety, reminds us that there is a further possibility: affirm the individual but explore an alternative response.

Options

'So what might you do?' 'What possibilities present themselves?' 'Where can we go from here?' Potential courses of action, or Options, need to be drawn out in some detail. This is the third component of GROW model coaching, and will certainly feature regularly in any ongoing accompanying relationship. 'What might you do, in recognition of those realities, in pursuit of those goals or desired outcomes?' 'What else?' will be the accompanier's most reiterated question at this juncture. 'And what else?' 'And anything further?' 'Is that everything, would you say?' 'Is there anything more?' says Nancy Kline, in her book *Time to Think*.[37] Kline's basic assumption is that it is the role of the facilitator not to seek to provide answers, but to draw out every possible response from the individual concerned. She works on the further assumption that every person carries within themselves the solution to their own dilemma.

One of the joys of accompaniment in general, and coaching in particular, is the moment when the light goes on in the eyes of your colleague. 'What else could you do?' you ask. 'Well,' they say, 'I suppose I could speak to their boss/drop a hint/write an email...' Then the moment, 'Actually, why don't I just... call by, take them for a coffee, explain just why I feel the way I do?' and the light goes on, and you know in that instant that they will do exactly what they themselves have now identified as being the most productive/ honest/positive course of action. Your work is done; they have identified a solution that carries their own integrity. All you had to do was ask, ask again and keep asking!

Will

Finally, the Will component. Sometimes this is described as 'Way Forward' or even 'What now?' However, 'Will' captures that sense of determined commitment to cause that is most likely to culminate in positive action. 'So, what will you now do?' 'What does that suggest to you about the most positive next step?' 'Is there something that you would want to commit to taking action on, before we next meet?' One of the strengths of consistent accompaniment is the ability to maintain accountability. Important to note, however, is that the accompanied has no accountability to the coach or accompanier per se, but rather gives them permission to hold accountability to themselves for following through on their own decisions and commitments. This is a significant distinction and an important aspect of a healthy accompaniment relationship.

Summary and execution

The simplicity of the GROW model is a major part of its charm. It also makes it eminently communicable. It does, though, lay it open to critique. Real life is often not as reducible to simple models as some of us would like it to be.

When our initial team of coaches was trained and deployed in the Canterbury Diocese using this model, there was a modicum of resistance to what appeared to be an overly simplistic approach. (We would expect nothing less from a team of such thoughtful, sensitive and articulate individuals.) This mild display of cynicism lasted throughout the initial training, and I do admit to a degree of apprehension. However, and most tellingly, any resistance very quickly dispersed when the model was seen in action. At the end of the first round of engagements, reviews were conducted among the coaches. (They were coaches rather than accompaniers at this stage. That story comes a little later.) Those on the receiving end, the accompanied and local church leaders, were also consulted and together they overwhelmingly concurred that the GROW model had proved to be integral to the success of the project. Some coaches used the model overtly, explaining the process, using the headings and structuring their conversations around the model. Others described how their engagements were more free-flowing but nevertheless shaped by the need for clarity of purpose, description of context and challenge, exploration of potential responses and courses of action decided upon. In other words, goals, realities, options and will. We continue to use the model, to hold it lightly in some instances, but always to work within its scope.

Jesus and the GROW model

Finally, in this consideration of GROW as a model for accompaniment in general and coaching in particular, it is worth taking a further glance at the Gospel narratives. How does the one map on to the other? The accounts of Jesus himself, and of his engagements with his followers, yield up some fascinating further insights into the appropriateness of applying these lessons to Christian mission and ministry.

Jesus and clear objectives

In Luke 9:51, Jesus 'resolutely set out for Jerusalem'. In the King James translation, this reads as 'steadfastly set his face'. This more than echoes Isaiah 50:7, 'Therefore I have set my face like flint.' This in turn reflects the sentiment of Psalms 57:7 and 108:1: 'My heart, O God, is steadfast [fixed].' Here is a messianic determination to pursue vocation. Jesus demonstrates his underlying sense of motivating purpose, or in coaching terms, 'goal'.

Earlier in the record, there is further evidence of Jesus setting priorities and acting accordingly. In Mark 1:38, the disciples urge Jesus to continue his well-received Capernaum ministry. He replies that he will in fact prioritise moving on to other locations, rather than simply further ministry in the same place. When told that 'everyone is looking for you' (v. 37), he replies, 'Let us go somewhere else – to the nearby villages – so that I can preach there also. That is why I have come.' Clear aspiration leads to determined priorities, which in turn shape decisions.

Incidentally, this reads as a delightful outworking of what Stephen R. Covey describes as 'being proactive', or 'starting with the end in mind' and 'putting first things first'. These are the first three life habits as delineated in his book *The 7 Habits of Highly Effective People*, which is a much-loved text from a coaching perspective.[38]

For Jesus, the priorities, or life goals, that appear to shape his sense of vocation and mission are crystallised during his wilderness retreat, his fasting and his temptations. Described by Mark in one sentence, this episode is treated at greater length by Matthew and Luke. In all three synoptic accounts, it sits between the description of his baptism and the start of the Galilean ministry. It is determinative. This is who he is. This is what he does. This is why he is here and what he sets himself, unswervingly, to accomplish. It was here that Jesus' identity as God's 'beloved son' was stress-tested and affirmed. He defines himself in relationship to his Father, a relational messiah serving a relational God.

When Jesus subsequently invites the fishermen, Simon, Andrew and then more, to become 'fishers of men' he begins consciously to draw others into the outworking of his life-shaping vision. Jesus sets objectives, clarifies outcomes and then multiplies accompaniment.

Jesus and facing realities

It could be argued that most of the story that unfolds in the Gospels is an object lesson in facing realities. With Simon Peter as a prime example, we can follow Jesus as he takes him on a journey of self-discovery. From disturbing personal insight, 'Go away from me, Lord; I am a sinful man!' (Luke 5:8) to unsustainable aspiration, 'Lord, if it's you… tell me to come…' (Matthew 14:28); from embarrassing blunder, 'Get behind me, Satan' (Mark 8:33) to incalculable challenge, 'Whoever does not carry their cross and follow me cannot be my disciple' (Luke 14:27), Peter confronts more reality in short order than most of us would fear to see in a lifetime. Jesus consistently calls the bluff of his followers. 'Do you now believe?' he probes in John 16:31, when the disciples claim at last to understand what is being told to them. If a coaching relationship requires an ability to be ruthlessly honest about context, and a readiness to hold uncertainty, while simultaneously looking for further options, then Jesus is once again 'the way'.

Jesus and reviewing options

'Do you also wish to go away?' (John 6:67, NRSV). 'Whoever has ears to hear, let them hear' (Mark 4:9) 'Won't you first sit down and estimate the cost?' (Luke 14:28). Jesus, through teaching, example, parable and miracle, gently but consistently confronts the disciples with options for life choices. He does not coerce, and neither does he prescribe a template for following him. Each one is invited to discover and embrace his own destiny. 'What is that to you?' Jesus says to Peter, when questioned about the discipleship of another (John 21:22) 'You must follow me.'

Jesus and will

John's account in the closing lines of the fourth Gospel takes us deeply and personally into the accompanying relationship between Jesus and Peter. It feels clumsy and a little crass to try to impose a contemporary coaching model on to such an intimate exchange between these two men. But the Gospel writer has already intruded, and indeed has been candid, in revealing his own motives for selecting the material that he uses ('… these are written that you may believe,' John 20:31). 'Do you love me?' Jesus asks of Peter, not once but three times. This is nothing if not 'will'. What will you do, Peter, with all that has been invested in you? How will you now respond to the journey that we have been on together? 'Feed my sheep' (John 21:17), 'Go and make disciples' (Matthew 28:19) and, 'when you have turned back, strengthen your brothers' (Luke 22:32).

Do we think that Jesus sets out to use a four-quadrant coaching model when shaping the lives of his followers? Not even for a moment. But that's not the point. The pressing question for us is, 'Can the insights of a GROW model, now so familiar to many in our contemporary society, be pressed into the service of mission in a way that is congruent with gospel values?' It looks very much as if they can.

My personal application

One of the most significant moments in my own discipleship journey came about not when I discovered one of the foundational biblical doctrines, 'All have sinned' or 'He died for all' or even 'If anyone is in Christ, he is a new creation'. Rather it was hearing, 'Come, follow me'.

I had been selling personal accident insurance for a while. Having failed to make the grade as a jockey, and after filling in time selling fruit and veg, I was temporarily earning quite a lot more than should have been possible for someone who had left school at 15 without a single qualification. The issue for me was that it proved deeply unsatisfying. The money helped, but it was earned persuading people to buy something that was not good value, and which they probably didn't need anyway. It was not just that I wanted rescuing out of a pit of despair, but more that I needed clarity about what really motivated me. My fresh encounter with Jesus would lead to motivation, direction, purpose: it would clarify goals and help me face realities, discover options and set out on a journey.

Your personal reflection

Time now to ask some specific coaching questions of yourself.

- GOALS: What would you most like to improve on, to make progress in, to achieve, right now? What would that look like, if you had to sum it up in one clear, simple sentence?
- REALITIES: What are the sheer practicalities of life currently impeding the pursuit of that aspiration?
- OPTIONS: What simple, believable, practical steps could you take to move forward from here? What else? Anything more?
- WILL: Who might you talk this through with? What action will you now take? By when?

7

Relational accompaniment: developing individuals

The road more travelled

The foundational Genesis story tells us that all human life is motivated by a drive towards relationship, fruitfulness and destiny (Genesis 1:28). That drive is constantly thwarted by the harsher realities of life (Genesis 3:14–19). Aspiration and disappointment are the counterpoints of the human score. Some inner sense tells us that life could be, ought to be, better, more fulfilling, than it actually is. What to do about that contradiction becomes a central theme of human experience.

When M. Scott Peck wrote *The Road Less Travelled* in 1978,[39] he was tapping into and helping to stimulate a massive upsurge in popular psychology and its application to the search for a fulfilled life. The book has sold more than five million copies to date. There is nothing new in the search for a better way of living. Sometime around 350 BC, Aristotle coined or at least popularised the concept of *eudaimonia* or 'flourishing', as the sum of human aspiration. Samuel Smiles is credited with having written the first self-help book of the modern era, appropriately titled *Self-Help*, published in 1859. Norman Vincent Peale joined the party in 1953 with the publication of *The Power of Positive Thinking*.[40]

There are many thousands more books that could be cited, but these titles are among the most significant, by virtue of their worldwide sales. Together they provide something of a platform for further exploration into the quest for human flourishing. The central theme of all these works is facing up to life's realities, taking responsibility for who you are and how you are, and cracking on. While there may not be much more new to say, there are some amazingly inventive ways of saying it, and it seems to bear repetition. The journey continues.

NLP takes to the stage

It was into the world of positive thinking, self-help and burgeoning aspiration that neuro-linguistic programming (NLP) was born. It is very much a product of late twentieth-century west-coast USA. NLP attempts to provide a practical structure to life-enhancing thought patterns. As a discipline, it offers fascinating, simple, but profound insights into the realm of personal psychology. Its approach is almost entirely pragmatic. It acknowledges what has gone before, but without wanting either to endorse or to take issue. 'What works' is of greater interest than why it works. It is a tool of more interest to the practitioner than the theorist.

Steve Bavister and Amanda Vickers suggest that NLP is 'a science, a process, a study, a model, a set of procedures, a manual, a system, an attitude, a strategy, a technology'.[41] They describe it more simply as 'applied psychology'.

NLP is predicated on the understanding that all the information we receive is processed by the brain, where it is codified by language and symbols. As we become more aware of what we think, how we think, how we process information, then we can increasingly take more control of our responses, actions and outcomes. This takes us beyond 'Let's aspire to the best' (Aristotle), 'Life is tough' (Peck) and 'Be more positive' (Peale). It goes a little deeper into 'What do you really want?', 'What are the specific challenges you currently face?' and 'What is the best achievable outcome in your present circumstances?' And, more importantly, 'What is the story that you are telling yourself right now?' and 'How would your world be different if you changed that narrative?' (And isn't the concept of

Christian conversion largely about changing your life narrative to a God-centred story of relational accompaniment?)

One of the earliest developers of NLP, Richard Bandler, famously asked why some therapists were more effective in facilitating change in their patients than others. 'What is the difference that makes the difference?' Bandler questioned, observed and then implemented what he learned. NLP came to birth simply by modelling the best practice of skilled therapists. In this way, Bandler and others like him went on to develop a range of psychological tools that could be easily transferred and safely used. NLP practitioners were for the most part the inheritors of that road, now increasingly travelled. In their role as coaches, they were enabled to effect significant and lasting change in the lives of their clients.

Personal disclosure

It was my experience first of being accompanied, then as an accompanier and finally as a trained 'GROW model' coach that fired my imagination to pursue training and accreditation in NLP.[42] This is not essential to the role of accompaniment, but it adds tools, insights and practices that have proved to be in accordance with our values. None of the other members on the teams with which I work is currently trained in this discipline, so in that regard it is not integral. However, it does inform my own approach, and has helped to shape the facilitating that has been offered to the wider team. It looks like this.

The four pillars of NLP

Steve Bavister and Amanda Vickers, in *Teach Yourself NLP*, cited above, describe the key elements of NLP as four pillars. This language is shared by many other writers on the subject, dating back to the originators, John Grinder and Richard Bandler.[43] They describe it this way:

Clarified outcomes

Clarified outcomes are foundational to coaching and accompaniment with NLP. 'What are you after?' 'What would that look like?' 'What would it feel like?' 'What would it sound like?' 'How would you know that you had reached that goal?' 'How would life be different for you if you were to achieve this outcome?' 'What implications would that have for other areas of your present life?' 'What would need to change?' 'What might you lose if you achieved that outcome?' The first pillar is about moving beyond vagueness and arriving at honesty, specificity and detailed ownership of future possibilities insofar as they lie within your own area of influence.

Sensory acuity

That leads neatly to the second pillar, which is sensory acuity. This describes the ability to become increasingly aware of input via the five senses. 'What associations exist with what you are now experiencing?' 'What memories are triggered?' 'How does that influence your interpretation of events?' 'How has this sensory input shaped your perception?' 'How does that influence your current mental state?' And, ultimately, 'What effect is that having on your ability to make sound judgements and effective choices?'

This pillar is built on what Grinder and Bandler called the 'meta-model'. In the simplest terms, this model provides a picture of information coming into the brain via the five senses. There it is processed through filters of past experiences and unexamined assumptions about self and the world. This in turn colours how the input is mapped on to the brain, producing a mental state (of excitement, depression, fear or opportunity, for example). Finally comes the realisation that this is what prompts our moods, attitudes, actions and outcomes. Becoming more aware of this process and its results is potentially life-transforming. That is the second pillar.

Rapport

The third pillar concerns creating rapport between coach and client, and more generally in functional relationships in the everyday arena. What is the most effective way of understanding another person? How best do we share someone else's perception of the world? What aids effective listening, deeper engagement and the best possibility of being a useful friend? Here we assume that the closest we can get to understanding another is to develop ways of seeing the world as they do. Only then can we fully engage with their fears and aspirations. Here, NLP offers tools for interpreting the preferred language models of our friends. Do they talk about 'the way I see it'? Or would they more often say, 'It feels to me'? Perhaps they favour mechanical language: 'I think it works like this'. Whichever it is, mirroring their preferred vocabulary is as effective in facilitating rapport as is the mirroring of body language (a skill long valued in counselling circles).

Incidentally, it is probably around this third pillar that any disquiet with NLP arises. I trained alongside health workers, personnel officers and charity executives who would use these new skills to better serve their clientele. I also trained with sales-force bosses and business executives who might equally use the same insights to better position themselves in the marketplace and persuade potential customers to buy their products.

Flexible response

The final foundation is flexible response. What do you do when more of the same isn't working? How do we develop, in ourselves and others, a greater facility for creative and innovative response? The underlying insight here is that the initiative in any given situation will always rest with the one who is most able to adapt. This is an evolutionary principle that has served us well so far, but is not always easily observed or acknowledged. For the Christian mission accompanier, this is a highly relevant factor, both for ourselves and for the others with whom we work. Trying to address new questions with old answers is endemic in the church. Much of the frustration that an accompanier meets in working with church leaders arises from the pressure to do what we have always done, only with even greater effort. (Remember the question, 'And what else could you do?' from our GROW-model coaching. There are always other possibilities!)

The pillars in practice

The principles described by the four pillars, the areas of study on which they are built and the insights that they convey are of immediate and far-reaching use to the coach and accompanier. Their application in practice has proved of measurable benefit.

It also gives language to and helps us to describe some of the pattern of befriending and discipling that Jesus demonstrates in the Gospels. (Please note that there is no suggestion that Jesus was somehow a clandestine NLP practitioner. The argument here is that these insights accord well with Jesus' ministry, and do not in any way clash with gospel values. They can provide a language, a model and practice that may facilitate a more effective discipling than we have achieved without them.) Before that, one further NLP tool deserves more detailed exploration.

Logical levels

There is one NLP tool in particular that illustrates well the application to accompaniment (and incidentally to the pattern of Jesus' engagement with his friends). Robert Dilts, an early developer of NLP, has built on the work of anthropologist Gregory Bateson to produce the model known as 'logical levels'.[44]

Diagram 4: Logical levels

As a means of communicating quickly what is a much more detailed concept, I offer here the fictional account of a young man who I will call 'Toby the tea boy'.

Environment

On his first day at work, Toby needs to know where the kitchen is, how to locate the kettle and in which cupboard the cups are housed. This is his 'environment', and the foundational base of the learning pyramid that this model describes. He simply needs information, and anyone who has access to it can pass it on.

Behaviour

As a next step, Toby needs to understand the 'behaviour' that is required of him. On arrival each morning, he is required to put the kettle on, get the cups out and start the process of making the tea. These are simple actions and can be quickly learned from anyone who has previously mastered them.

Skill

Beyond that, Toby needs to acquire skills. He needs to know that it's best to take the pot to the kettle, rather than the other way around. He should warm the pot first. Furthermore, there are interpersonal skills that will improve his effectiveness. Some people in the firm prefer Earl Grey to Breakfast tea. Knowing who takes sugar will greatly enhance his reception. These are skills that can and should be acquired. Here he moves from mere information, through mechanical actions, to specific abilities that will need practising and honing.

Those three levels form the bottom half of the pyramid (see diagram 4). He requires information, instruction and training to progress through the levels. Now it becomes even more interesting.

In the top half of the pyramid are three further levels. These are not the kind of qualities that can be mechanically conveyed. Now something further, deeper, more potentially life-changing is required.

Beliefs

At the next level, Toby shapes his inner beliefs about the work he is doing and about its place in the bigger picture of life. If he says to himself, 'This is a rubbish job', then his inner attitude will soon manifest itself in his approach to work, to his colleagues and to life in general. If other people contribute towards this negative view of his role, and its lack of significance, then he will be reaffirmed in a less-than-helpful outlook and demeanour.

If, however, in sharp contrast, he was told and believed that this was an amazing contribution towards the well-being of his colleagues, then the world would become a different and better place. Providing a cheering cup at the start of a day's work might just make all the difference to the performance, output and general well-being of Toby's colleagues. If he believes this to be true, if this more positive inner discourse feeds into his core outlook, then the world changes for him and for those around him. Beliefs matter, and their effect goes way beyond the private sphere.

Identity

Beyond this, Toby shapes his own self-identity. 'I *am* the tea boy', not just 'I'm the person whose task is to make the tea'. Toby can again nurture more negative or positive influences, through the nature of his self-awareness. 'I'm *just* the tea boy' is one thing. 'I'm the dispenser of good cheer in this place' is quite another. What does he see when he looks in the mirror? Who does he see? How does he understand his place within the grand scheme of things? The lowest of the low, or a young man on a mission?

Vision

Finally, the top of the pyramid is reached at the pinnacle of mission, passion and vision. 'For this purpose have I come into the world.' Toby's destiny lies in being the most effective, the best, the cheeriest tea boy that it is possible for him to be! Ultimately, this is what will shape Toby's thoughts and actions all the way down and through the pyramid. This is what will get him out of bed in the morning. This is what will motivate him to remember to warm the pot and brew the tea to perfection. Depending on his sense of mission, the identification of his passion and the shape of his vision, Toby has the potential to change the world, or at least to change his world and that of those around him. What relationships might be saved because a discontented individual is given pause for thought by the kindly ministrations of a considerate tea boy? What business might thrive, providing services and employment for thousands, because of the calming influence of a superbly executed refreshment break? What difference might a well-served cup of tea make to tense political negotiations at the very highest level? Toby could indeed change the world.

On the very day that I first taught this model to a gathering of colleagues, I read a particularly striking story in the local press. It described an interview with a newly appointed primary-school head teacher. The new head had started her career at this very school, as one of the dinner ladies, and had worked her way onwards from there. As a potential head teacher, I guess that she made a particularly great dinner lady.

The applied pyramid

To understand the relevance of the logical levels pyramid is to glimpse the possibilities inherent in a coaching, mentoring, discipling, accompanying relationship. This is NLP in practice, informing, shaping and enhancing development in others.

In the lower half of the pyramid lie the traditional areas of instruction, training and equipping. Here are the very practical tasks and responsibilities upon which any work or ministry must be built. The qualities in the upper half of the levels, however, are beyond mere instruction. This is the arena of motivation, the location of life-changing vocation. This is a journey that cannot be taught. It can only be accompanied. To walk with an individual through developing beliefs, clarifying identity and the emergence of life-changing passions is to experience the highest privilege that life affords. (Or perhaps that's just my own belief, self-identity and passion?)

A brief tour around motivation

Helping our friends, colleagues and clients to identify their own driving motivation will lie at the heart of what we contribute as accompaniers. Jesus called it 'fine pearls' when teasing his listeners with an extended metaphor on the subject of what we would sell our lives for (Matthew 13:45–46).

George New and David Cormack, in *Why Did I Do That?*,[45] write about extrinsic and intrinsic motivation. They quickly dispense with extrinsic (outside, external) factors and concentrate on inner motivation. The classic treatise on motivation at work was *One*

More Time: How do you motivate employees?, written by Frederick Herzberg in 1968.[46] His thesis was that motivation to improve, perform, achieve and fulfil always comes from internal, intrinsic factors. External factors, such as work environment, salary levels, bonus schemes and promotions, if absent, certainly do contribute to demotivation, but when present are of much less significance than intrinsic factors in changing behaviour.

We need to find the values in what we do. Herzberg's work shows that simply offering more money rarely leads to improved performance. It is when we can articulate our values, and then work in congruence with them, that we are motivated best. It is here that we can help our accompanied friends to uncover those hidden springs. We can be subtle but persistent in asking those revelatory questions. 'What would that do for you, if you achieved that particular goal?' 'Why is that important, would you say?' 'Can you put into words exactly how that would make a difference?' And then you ask the same questions, in a slightly different form, of each subsequent answer, until you get closer, much closer, to the buried roots of the matter.

Jesus, logical levels and contemporary discipling

If Toby can be accompanied to the pinnacle of his career as a tea boy, what might that say to us in our desire to walk the heights with Jesus? What of our contemporary vocation to be disciples? What of our call to model discipleship, and to invite others to join us on the journey? What of accompaniment as an outworking of the great commission? What, indeed, of the logical levels as a model for Christian discipleship? What light does accompaniment shed and what may we glean for our commitment to journeying with others?

Foundations of the pyramid

Jesus 'sent [the disciples] two by two ahead of him to every town and place where he was about to go,' says Luke 10:1. Jesus offers basic-level information and behavioural guidance. 'Do not judge one another', 'Forgive one another'. 'Wash one another's feet' (John 13:14), he tells them in the upper room. Induction into the basic behaviours of discipleship accords with the lower half of the logical levels pyramid. This is simple training. In just such a way, Jesus instructs his disciples in the basic practices of following him. This much accords with the most straightforward induction into new tasks and responsibilities. There will always be a foundational instructional level to a life of following Jesus.

It becomes life-changing, however, in the next phase, as we move through the upper sectors of the logical levels. Here, reappraised beliefs and values prepare the way for a change of perceived identity, culminating in a definitive and life-shaping vision.

Values

'What good thing must I do?' asks Tom Wright in the opening sentence of *Virtue Reborn*.[47] In that book, the author suggests that the search for a satisfying life ethic (which he traces back historically as far as Aristotle's *eudaimonia*) is the basic human drive that is answered by the Christian gospel. The logical levels model shows that behaviours will ultimately flow from values and beliefs. The days are long gone when we thought that we could simply teach, inform and instruct upcoming generations into meaningful Christian faith. 'Because I say so' works for only so long in the parent-to-child (transactional analysis) model. The 19th-century Sunday school movement contributed a great deal to national life in Britain. What it didn't do, and still won't, is disciple a nation in the life of Jesus. Adult-to-adult relational accompaniment, in pursuit of awakened and espoused values, looks much more like the New Testament pattern.

'Are you not much more valuable than they?' Jesus asks rhetorically, referring to birds of the air. 'Seek first his kingdom and his righteousness' (Matthew 6:26, 33). The disciples are challenged in the first instance by the espoused and lived values evidenced in the life and ministry of Jesus himself. Jesus lives his identity and vocation. In his wilderness temptations, he has very deliberately rejected the motivations of power and achievement. He has even resisted the possibility of achieving his aims through popular acclaim. He has clarified his values at the outset. He has committed to live by those values. He does that with such compelling integrity that it awakens the wonder and fascination of his followers. He deliberately provokes their deeper interest, and stimulates more and more revealing self-reflection. Again and again, in parable and story, in action and interpretation, Jesus invites his friends to re-examine their own lives and re-evaluate their own underlying beliefs.

Identity

To hear the words 'You are my Son' (Mark 1:11) was a defining moment at the outset of Jesus' ministry. 'When you pray, say "Father"' (Luke 11:2) does the same thing for his followers. 'Instead, I have called you friends' (John 15:15) enhances the growing self-awareness of the disciples. 'Children of God' and 'friends of Jesus' will see the world in a very different light from 'struggling fishermen' or 'socially excluded tax collectors'.

'Who actually are you?' is a great question for a coach to ask. 'How do you define yourself?' 'What is it that specifically shapes your self-identity?' This is the penultimate level of the pyramid model, and it profoundly influences every level below. The function of baptism, in the liturgical and sacramental life of the Christian church, is surely to secure this very identity – raised to life with Christ, one with him and part of the body. 'I am baptised,' thundered Martin Luther in the face of spiritual doubt and inner conflict. It matters how we see ourselves and it matters how we facilitate that self-awareness in others.

Vision

'I am the light of the world' (John 9:5) was vocation enough for Jesus. 'You are the light of the world' (Matthew 5:14) works similarly for his friends. The pinnacle of the logical levels pyramid lies at the point at which an individual can articulate their life purpose.

There is a Japanese word for the motivational heartbeat at the centre of life. The word is *ikigai* and it has found its way into the coaching and mentoring lexicon. It is variously described as 'what gets you out of bed in the morning' or 'what makes life worthwhile'. Dr Steve Peters in his book *The Chimp Paradox*[48] uses the concept of 'the life stone' for the same purpose. It's all about knowing who you are and what you're for. It's the touchstone by which every other commitment, priority and decision is measured. One of the most famous of holocaust survivors, Vicktor Frankl, says (quoting from Friedrich Nietzsche), 'Those who have a "why" to live, can bear with almost any "how".'[49]

That takes us right back to the foundational motivation behind the goals of the GROW model. It recapitulates the clarified objectives of NLP. 'That is why I have come,' says Jesus (Mark 1:38). The individual, church, deanery or diocese that can answer that question with clarity and passion is well on its way. It's the ultimate purpose of accompaniment. It's the outworking of all mission. It's the fulfilment of discipleship. It's an aspiration to a changed culture where the accompanied accompany others, the coached coach and disciples disciple disciple-making disciples. 'As the Father has sent me, I am sending you,' says Jesus (John 20:21). What more could we possibly need? Except perhaps the presence of a comforter and the power of an accompanying Holy Spirit.

Your personal reflection

Before reading on, take some time to work through this model for yourself. This may require more than one sitting.

- What are the practical skills that you need right now, in order to navigate the next stretch of your life's journey?
- What further information do you need to seek out?
- Who might help you with that?

Then revisit those earlier questions about your deepest underlying motivations.

- What are the values that in practice shape your behaviour?
- Where did they come from?
- How are they actually expressed in the hustle and bustle of your everyday responsibilities?
- What would an alien observer conclude from your actions, your priorities, your leisure and your finances about what actually matters most to you?
- How do you see yourself? What determines your identity? How is that expressed?
- What is the story that you are telling yourself, about yourself, right now?
- Finally, what are the passions that drive you forward and urge you onwards?
- Who could help you talk this through and work this out further?

8

Relational accompaniment: the honing of an idea

Relational accompaniment is deeply rooted in the nature of God. It is an incarnated principle embedded in the essence of the gospel. It is, in a multiplicity of ways, illustrated throughout church history. For those of us working with the concept of relational accompaniment in the early years of the 21st century, however, there are three clear strands of recent history that will help us to understand how we have arrived at where we are today.

Strand one: world mission – the big picture

The world of Christian mission changed dramatically during the course of the 20th century. In 1910, the major Protestant denominations that were engaged in mission held a massive conference in Edinburgh. Two years later, in 1912, the first edition of *Missionary Methods: St Paul's or ours?* by Anglican priest Roland Allen was published after first-hand research in China, India, Africa and Canada. In 1923, a young Chinese Christian by the name of Ni Tuosheng published his first written works (the man later to become known worldwide as Watchman Nee). In 1929, Sadhu Sundar Singh set out on his final missionary journey from his home in India into the foothills of Tibet.

What these seemingly random events have in common is their illustration of a significant shift in missional emphasis. This is the movement away from 'mission to', towards 'mission with'.

The Edinburgh Conference called for greater indigenisation. Roland Allen urged mission societies to move swiftly towards calling and releasing local leaders for local churches. Nee and Singh, in China and India respectively, were initially influenced by incoming, paternalistic mission structures. Now they were part of a movement that was learning to prioritise the local contextual work of its own people in their own culture. Mission and discipling were becoming less authoritarian and more releasing. Mission was becoming less imported and more local. The role of the missionary was being redefined as less of a messenger from a far country and more of a companion in this one. Mission was becoming accompaniment and the missionary an accompanier.

So, when Vincent Donovan wrote *Christianity Rediscovered* in 1978,[50] he was giving voice not only to his own discoveries in Tanzania but to the clarifying insights of 20th-century Christian mission. Donovan was a Roman Catholic missionary to the Maasai tribes during the 1960s and beyond. His book tells the story of his 15 years of that work in Tanzania. This book, more than any, recounts the shift in missional emphasis. In it, hè describes his own initial failures, and that of the missionary assumptions in which he had been schooled. Trying to relate a Westernised, institutionalised version of Christianity wasn't proving very successful in rural Africa.

Christianity Rediscovered has become a classic of missional thinking and practice. Donovan is much quoted by the present generation of pioneers and Fresh Expressions practitioners. He speaks of the missional journey undertaken together. This most definitely is 'mission with' and not simply 'mission to'. He talks about a shared relationship that enables transformation in both accompanied and accompanier. Genuine, biblical, kingdom mission will change both parties. It will be a journey of discovery for all involved. 'You must have the courage to go with them to a place that neither you nor they have ever been before.' This is potentially life-changing for all. Mission must carry equal risk for both parties. Mission, if it is to be true to a relational God, has to be relational, in an adult-to-adult mode.

Strand two: local mission – the specific picture

We turn now from the big picture of world mission to one particular local story. In the Introduction, I referred to the practice of mission accompaniment in the Diocese of Canterbury. This is my own story and it is shaped significantly by my own positive experiences, both of being accompanied and of accompanying others.

You can't get very far in telling the story of mission accompaniment in the UK during the past 30 years without coming across the massive contribution made by Bob and Mary Hopkins. Bob and Mary are the founders of Anglican Church Planting Initiatives (ACPI). They have provided significant resources and networking for those engaged in the church-planting movement since its years below the radar in the 1980s. Since then, they have almost certainly accompanied more leaders and missional projects than anyone else across the church, including bishops, archdeacons and diocesan advisors. Together with George Lings (the founder and director of the research unit at the Church Army's Sheffield Centre) they have held the story of planting, pioneering and Fresh Expressions in and beyond the Church of England.

As part of the leadership team at St Thomas Crookes in Sheffield, Bob and Mary participated in setting up a large-scale coaching programme, which came to be known as '3DM'. Here the concepts of discipleship, coaching, mentoring and accompaniment were being explored together as an integral part of that church's journey towards becoming a missional community, and not just a centre where worshippers gathered on a Sunday.

In chapter 4, I laid out part of the story of HARVEST New Anglican Church, and how it provided us with an opportunity to build church on relational principles. That was initially a painful journey and one that was not well understood by the wider church at the time. Bob and Mary came alongside my wife, Eunice, and me as we trod that tough path together. We were not consciously accessing mission accompaniment as a principle, but simply reaching out for the personal warmth and encouragement needed in such a context.

Bob's book on coaching, *Coaching for Missional Leadership*,[51] written with Freddy Hedley out of his experience with 3DM and countless other personal engagements, spells out the very practical skills and practices that he and Mary have applied, again and again, to succeeding generations of pioneers. 'For coaching to be effective, it relies on the strength of this relationship between the coach and the missional leader,' write Bob and Freddy.[52]

When the leadership of Canterbury Diocese gave permission for the setting up of HARVEST New Anglican Church in 1998, a protocol was established that we as leaders would be accompanied. A small group was established, chaired by the archdeacon (on behalf of the bishop). Bob and Mary were appointed by the Archdeacon of Canterbury to serve on that group. What none of us realised at the time was that this was establishing a principle later to be enshrined in all newly authorised pioneer projects. What had been pioneered on the margins is now coming into the mainstream.

The publication of the *Mission-Shaped Church* report in 2004 marked a definitive turning point in the story of new forms of church. HARVEST, and our experience there, was included in the report. The experience of many other, equally ambitious, ventures was similarly brought to light. Many of us discovered that our seemingly lone path was not in fact unique.

Along with formal recognition came the promise and commitment of a newly created legal instrument which would secure the place of what were now being called 'Fresh Expressions of Church' within the historic structures of the Church of England. The concept of a Bishop's Mission Order (BMO) was born. The BMO (which HARVEST helped to formulate, and was the first to receive) required that every Fresh Expression, thus authorised, should have an appointed 'Bishop's Visitor'.

While not requiring the Bishop's Visitor to be in all cases the actual accompanier, it did establish the value and need for such a role. The Church of England's own guide to the BMO (Bishop's Mission Orders)[53] states that the role of the Visitor is to 'provide a key element in the structures of support, advice and encouragement, alongside coaching or mission accompaniment'. It goes on to say that 'it is the Visitor's job to ensure that such accompaniment is in place'.

To the dioceses and beyond

Such is the impact of Bob and Mary's accompaniment skill that when Phil Potter (leader of the national Fresh Expressions team) put together the first round of Inter-Diocesan Learning Communities (IDLC) in 2013, it fell to Bob to facilitate the experiment. A significant amount of Church Commissioners' funding was allocated to bringing together the bishops and senior teams from eight different dioceses for an accompanied process of mission planning, priority setting and strategic innovation. These teams met together every nine months or so, over a three-year period. So positive was the response, and so strategic the outcomes, that the Church Commissioners took over the process in order to roll it out further across the Church of England. They have recruited not only facilitators for the process but also accompaniers to continue the learning. Relational accompaniment, which starts out as an aspect of the nature of God, has finally reached the upper echelons of the Anglican Church.

Strand three: 'Bridges of Hope'

The third of the three strands mentioned in the opening paragraph of this chapter (in addition to lessons from the big picture of world mission and the local experience of pioneer projects such as HARVEST) arises from the work of Churches Together in Britain and Ireland (CTBI). The CTBI project Building Bridges of Hope was trailed briefly in chapter 1, 'The case for accompaniment'.

The Building Bridges of Hope project was brought about by a coalition of church leaders from Britain and Ireland. Their imaginations had been fired at a European mission conference held in Potsdam, Germany, in the mid 1990s.[54] Among the speakers at that event were the missionary bishop, Lesslie Newbiggin of the Church of South India, and Dr Gerhard Linn, a leading German ecumenical theologian. Bishop Newbiggin spoke of the need for local congregations to rediscover their primary role as missional communities. Dr Linn recounted the story of thriving East German congregations which had flourished despite the severe restrictions placed upon them by the prevailing communist regime. The concept of the accompanied congregation was highlighted and the attending leaders wanted to discover more.

An initial phase of the project was established under the leadership of Dr Ron Ram, a Methodist layman. Research was carried out in a range of congregations across Britain and Ireland, covering every major denomination, in 40 separate locations. A willingness to be accompanied was identified as one of the most essential elements of congregational flourishing. Janice Price, Executive Secretary of the Global Mission Network of CTBI, put it this way:

> One core value, however, stood out above all others in the journey of growth: an openness to receive the insights of the skilled outsider. Popularly known as mission accompaniment, this openness was evident in all growing church communities.[55]

The next phase of the Building Bridges of Hope project required the recruiting and training of a team of 35 mission accompaniers. These men and women were then matched to 35 churches, religious communities and denominational projects across Britain and Ireland for a five-year accompaniment. Accompaniers visited their projects every two or three months. Accompaniers and accompanied kept a log of all visits, questions raised, issues explored and progress made. The accompaniers and the representatives of the teams with which they were working met annually for a conference to monitor progress and examine specific learning issues.

The previously mentioned *Journey into Growth* was published in 2007, telling the story and identifying lessons learned. *Mission Accompaniment* by Philip Walker (2005)[56] tells the same story but from the perspective of an outside and independent observer. Philip Walker briefly tells the story of four accompanied projects before concluding,

> I was convinced that outside help was necessary before I began writing, but the more I have thought through and written, the more I am convinced that we all need a Jethro or Paul to mentor us as Jesus would. All of us as church leaders need accompaniers, just as individuals – especially new converts – need them, but so do churches and organizations. BBH has something valuable to teach us, but only as it becomes part of mainstream church life.[57]

My experience, as one of the accompanied leaders whose story is told in both *Journey into Growth* and *Mission Accompaniment*, leads me firmly to echo that conclusion. Little wonder, then, that the concept and language of relational mission accompaniment commended themselves as a guiding principle to my subsequent work as Diocesan Mission and Growth Advisor in Canterbury. Drawing on all three of those strands – developments in world mission, local lessons learned and the researched experience of BBH – we turn now to a more detailed account.

On, then, to my story of life in Canterbury Diocese. On to the arcane world of a growing and declining, functioning and non-functioning, flying and flapping, contemporary Church of England diocese. How could we facilitate a flourishing missional life across the working (and non-working) relationships? How could we change the culture? What might mission accompaniment achieve?

Your personal reflection

Before we continue:

- What of your own story?
- What are the influences on your own understanding of, and engagement in, mission?
- What is the working context in which you would most want to see those influences brought to bear?

9

Relational accompaniment: changing a culture

The impossible dream?

Can you change a culture? If by culture we mean 'the way we do things around here' then it looks like a tall order, if not an impossible dream. Culture is deep-rooted and all-pervasive. The culture of a nation is formed over centuries, millennia even. It is expressed in language, art, literature, song and folklore. It helps to define the nation. We assume that it has always been like this, and always will be. It is who we are.

The culture of a workplace, an office, a factory or a church is not quite so deep-rooted, but every bit as pervasive. 'You'll soon learn' is one of the most often-repeated phrases that a new colleague is likely to hear in the early days in a new working environment. 'That's not how we do things around here.' No one can quite remember how, when or why we got to do things that way. But that's how it is, so don't rock the boat.

Many a manager in the workplace or leader in a church has their heart broken trying to change a culture. This is where that famous, but elusive, phrase comes from: 'Culture eats strategy for breakfast.'

No one knows for certain where that saying originates. (It was probably the management guru Peter Drucker.) What is not disputed is the accuracy of the observation. Good ideas come and go. New initiatives burn brightly and then fade as quickly. What remains the same is the underlying culture, 'the way we do things around here'.

Churches, whole denominations even, hold debates, write reports, implement initiatives; there is never any shortage of bright ideas. What is needed, though, is culture change. We need sound theology; we need the practical application of tested psychological wisdom. We need flourishing individuals, being the best and bringing out the best. What we need are the insights, values and practices of relational mission accompaniment.

Looking in the mirror

There is a profound challenge at the heart of culture change. It is as uncomfortable as it is unavoidable. 'Be the change that you want to see' is a paraphrase of how Gandhi had put it. 'The Word became flesh and made his dwelling among us' is how John describes Jesus incarnating this life-changing truth (John 1:14). 'If it doesn't happen here, it won't happen anywhere' is how I most often express it, to myself and my colleagues. Unless we grow, unless we change, unless we live out the very principles that we are commending to others, then it's all whistling in the wind. Whatever we are trying to communicate, we the leaders, the communicators, the missionaries must be living examples, bearing the scars, embodying the principles and living the life.

Learning from the commercial world

It is ironic that senior church leadership is turning more and more to business models at a time when business is beginning to make dramatic discoveries of its own, in the opposite direction.

Reinventing Organizations is a 2014 publication by Frederic Laloux.[58] The subtitle, 'A guide to creating organizations inspired by the next stage of human consciousness', provides a hint to the slightly esoteric nature of its provenance. The fact that the Foreword is contributed by philosopher and mystic Ken Wilber says more. But, and this is the point, the book describes in some detail the emerging culture of twelve very real, very practical and very successful businesses in which the aspiration of human flourishing has come to replace the traditional goal of a pared-to-the-bone, profit-obsessed, hierarchical structure.

The case studies include a Dutch home-based healthcare service, a French brass foundry, a German publicly funded school, a multinational engineering company and more predictably several USA-based organisations, covering (less predictably) tomato production, addiction recovery, energy distribution, mountain climbing equipment and of course the publication and dissemination of 'spiritual wisdom'. Laloux identifies three key characteristics at the heart of this emerging culture, which he characterises as 'self-management, wholeness and evolutionary purpose'. Behind the practices of these organisations and undergirding those key principles lies an aspiration for a relational human flourishing that sounds deeply familiar.

Again and again, Laloux describes company practices designed to provide safe space for employees to be more honest, more relational and more supportive than traditional structures allow. As a result, the individuals flourish, the company flourishes and the clients flourish.

One of his best examples concerns the Dutch home-care company Buurtzorg. The founder, Jos de Blok, describes how the organisation grew in ten years from one team of carers to 850 such teams. The workforce is 10,000 strong. The administrative back-up team is just 45 people. They employ 18 coaches, who are available on request to any of the teams needing help. Laloux poihts out how the culture of the organisation is embedded at absolutely every level. 'The only make-or-break factors are the worldview held by the top leadership,' he says, of all the organisations covered in the study.[59]

Laloux describes how the Buurtzorg teams are freed to form community among themselves:

Buurtzorg teams have no boss. All team members – typically ten to twelve people – are nurses. They deal with all the usual management tasks that arise in every team context: they set direction and priorities, analyse problems, make plans, evaluate people's performance and make the occasional tough decisions. Instead of placing these tasks on one single person – the boss – team members distribute these management tasks among themselves. The teams are effectively self-governing and self-organising.[60]

People are drawn to work in such settings because of the personal flourishing it enables. Asking questions about an individual worker's 'personal calling', Laloux says, 'Does the organisation's purpose resonate with me? Is this a place I feel called to work? What do I really feel called to do at this moment in my life? Will this place allow me to express my selfhood? Will it help me grow and develop?'[61] (No harm in pausing to ask yourself those questions right now. What will you do with, and about, the answers that you give?)

Laloux's book describes an aspiration towards the kind of human flourishing that churches can and should provide. Sadly, we are not often modelling the releasing relational accompaniment that should be our hallmark, and towards which even secular organisations are now striving. People are longing for an environment in which they can fulfil their highest calling. We can, and should, provide it.

The Canterbury tale: facing reality

The Church of England Diocese of Canterbury is not unusual. There are many mostly rural dioceses, with mostly smaller churches, mostly with a noble heritage, but now mostly working hard to make a significant impact on their communities.

'I'm just going through the motions.' 'This is not what I signed up to.' 'How soon can I retire?' These are genuine, heartbroken and heartbreaking quotes from friends and acquaintances gathered during my years of accompaniment work in Canterbury Diocese. It didn't take long for me to realise the true weight of pressure experienced by my clergy colleagues, and the profound need, not for another bright idea, but for culture change.

How could we accept such a depressing situation? What was it that Jesus promised? Life to the full? An easy burden and a light yoke? What were those relational insights? Human beings in supportive, life-enhancing, flourishing and functioning relation to one another? What does the coaching model promise? Clarified goals achieved with joy? What does NLP claim to be able to deliver? Identity, aspiration and life purpose fulfilled? What is the church called to do, to be, to model and to invite others into? Come on! If we can't do lasting culture change here, where can we do it?

Finding a way

Canterbury Diocese has 231 parishes grouped into 15 area deaneries. We simply didn't have the resources to provide accompaniment for every parish, so what could we do?

Like many great ideas whose time has come, relational accompaniment in the Diocese of Canterbury took off because of the convergence of several contributory factors. There was a diocesan secretary (the person responsible for the central resource team) desperate to make the team more effective and efficient. 'We need to break out of our silos and work in a much better-connected way' was how he would express that passion. Add to that a bishop determined to see the diocesan team structured as interconnected frameworks rather than separate departments. Those of us working on the ground knew perfectly well that we were only scratching the surface. So much more support, encouragement and help were needed. The aspiration was there. How could we deliver on it?

The rubber and the road

In the event, we identified three priorities. We could offer to accompany our Fresh Expressions of Church. We could commit to supporting that small number of parishes in receipt of mission grant money (for work that had been identified as having the greatest potential with the least resources). We could work with our 15 deaneries. The possibility of accompanying them was a bold aspiration, but it might just work. And it might help to change a culture.

Accompanying Fresh Expressions

One of the most influential contributions of the national Fresh Expressions team has been the provision of the *mission shaped ministry* course (*msm*). We quickly adopted it in Canterbury, working with ecumenical colleagues and in partnership with our sister diocese of Rochester. For all of us, it provided a positive stimulus to new forms of mission.

The year-long *msm* course, conducted in monthly sessions, is itself an accompanied journey. Individuals are dissuaded from attending the course on their own, and strongly encouraged to come as part of a team, either existing or potential. The *msm* experience fosters an appreciation of learning in community, and of being willing to reflect honestly together. It provides a context for teams to articulate aspirations and to be held gently accountable to their own espoused outcomes. *msm* is essentially a school for accompaniment.

Little wonder, then, that after *msm* those teams should look for and appreciate the opportunity for continued accompaniment. In much the same way that the Alpha Course has changed expectations of the faith journey, so *msm* helps to embed a desire for accompanied mission. They are both relational rather than didactic. In both courses, the foundations for an underlying shift in culture have already been laid.

So, in Canterbury Diocese, a small team of relational mission accompaniers was trained and deployed to carry that culture shift forward with pioneer teams fresh from the *msm* course.

Accompanying mission projects

The pot of money available to a diocese for the support of its struggling parishes is limited. Sound strategy suggests that those limited finances be directed towards the places with the greatest need and the highest potential. Might that be another strategy about to be eaten for breakfast by the prevailing culture? The far-reaching decision was taken that there would be no money without accompaniment. Every project in receipt of a grant would be allocated an accompanier. We recognised that throwing money was never going to be enough on its own. Particularly if, by so doing, we simply raised the expectation on an already harassed leader to be producing more and better measurable results. It was the perfect scenario for relational accompaniment. Ongoing support allied to clarification of goals, gentle accountability and a relational connection to the wider resource team would add up to the beginning of culture shift.

Accompanying deaneries

The biggest shift of all came in the commitment to accompaning deaneries.

Sadly, not every deanery sees itself as a meaningful missional unit. Local loyalty is, understandably, more often focused on the parish. In the days when almost every parish could boast its own vicar and vicarage, and church life was largely funded out of centrally held resources, that pattern was sustainable, if not a recipe for flourishing mission. In 1933, there were 403 paid clergy in the Diocese of Canterbury. In 2010, the number was down to 118. Currently, only about 18 per cent of parishes in the diocese have their own vicar; the rest are part of larger groupings under shared leadership. Like it or not, local churches need each other like never before. It looks as if the concept of deanery is an idea whose time has come.

Culture shift at the heart of the diocese

'Now I understand what a diocese is for,' said one deanery recipient of accompaniment. 'We no longer think of the diocese as "*them*",' said another. How did we get to that place?

Quite simply, it was as a result, not of one or two highly skilled individuals, but of a paradigm shift in the working of the central diocesan team. The Director of Communications, the Director of Education, the Deputy Director of Education, the Ministry Development Officer, the Children, Youth and Schools Advisor, the Stewardship Advisor, the Director of Communities and Partnership and the Mission and Ministry Executive Officer all came to the party. Each one was assigned to a deanery. By becoming deanery mission accompaniers alongside their existing specialist responsibilities, each one gained fresh insight into the life of the diocese, the entire team gaining a clearer understanding of the whole.

Towards a changed culture

It would be unrealistic to suggest that this pattern of working has become embedded at every level. It would be overly optimistic to suggest that the gains are irreversible. There are enough encouragements, however, to make it worthwhile taking stock and drawing lessons.

It began, developed and continues relationally. The Canterbury story of mission accompaniment is not one of a programme conceived, planned and delivered on schedule. This was not the subject of a discussion paper, carefully debated, pored over, corrected and voted on. It emerged. It grew. It came about through unfolding aspirations, ongoing working relationships and in a mishmash of structures. It grew between colleagues bearing a range of responsibilities at various levels in an institution bound by its history but increasingly desperate to find a better way of being. Most of the participants, accompaniers and accompanied, joined the story after observing and listening to colleagues. It was modelled, commended and adopted relationally.

The accompaniers do not operate as part of a hierarchical structure. From the start, it was made clear to all that accompaniment was not line management by another name. There was initially some concern that this might not be able to deliver robust change. Some feared that it would be overly directive; others that it would not be directive enough. The defining paragraph, which heads the subsequently produced documentation now given to all engaged in the process, reads:

> Accompaniment is the forming of a continuing relationship in pursuit of ever clarifying intentional outcomes. It includes support, encouragement, accountability, discernment and persistence.

The mention of accountability refers not to the deanery becoming beholden to the accompanier, but rather to the accompanier holding the deanery to its own agreed outcomes. Skilled accompaniers enable the deanery to clarify its own aspirations, to be realistic about its challenges, to explore its options and to commit to its vision. Goals, Realities, Options and Will – this is GROW-model coaching in a collegial, relational setting.

The accompaniers are themselves accompanied. 'If it doesn't happen here, it won't happen anywhere.' The diocesan team of accompaniers came to their task initially by being invited into the conversations of those who had begun the modelling. The team meetings and conversations were themselves a living example of colleagues learning and exploring together. These meetings now take the form of a 'learning set'. After an initial update and overview, one or more accompanier is given the opportunity to identify a particular challenge facing them in their work. This is related to the group, uninterrupted and without comment or question. Other team members are, however, listening, reflecting and writing questions on Post-it notes. After a strictly timed five-minute presentation of the issue, each listening colleague in turn asks the question they have noted. No advice is allowed! Questions that attempt to smuggle in good ideas are discouraged. The questions are for genuine elucidation, clarification and further reflection. The accompanier in the hot seat is under no obligation to respond to the Post-it questions, but may do if desired. No follow-up questioning is available. At the end of the round, the accompanier reflects on what has now come to light, in their own thinking, through pondering the questions. They are then encouraged to refine two or three specific actions that they will pursue as a result. These are written up, spoken aloud and handed back to the accompanier. There is a confidentiality protocol that no one is permitted to raise the issues thus disclosed and discussed, unless instigated by the accompanier themselves. This is condensed accompaniment. It is submitting to a continuing learning and growing process that has to be embraced by those wanting to facilitate the same experience in others.

Can we model that at every level of church life?

Taking stock

'Thank you for helping us to keep mission on the agenda while we have been facing such overwhelming structural and financial issues,' said one deanery leader.

'Who would have thought that we could achieve this level of cooperation?' said another.

'I still don't think the concept of deanery means much here,' said a third (included in the interests of integrity and balance).

Pause for thought

There are, however, some dissenting voices. Not everyone is convinced that the underlying philosophy of positivity, aspiration and goal-setting are firm enough foundations for healthy living, let alone specifically Christian mission.

All well and good, they say, to use relational, theological and spiritual language about our pursuit of growth and development. But hang on for a moment. Isn't there another, less positive, way of seeing all this? Aren't we buying into the world's view of success? Isn't our calling to self-giving rather than self-fulfilling? In picking up a coaching model, might we not be guilty of simply piling on the pressure to already overworked colleagues just to be more productive?

Time for us to take the challenge seriously and reflect on all that our critics might want to say.

Your personal reflection

- What culture are you a part of, which would benefit from a shift?
- What difference could you make by adopting relational missional values in your workplace or church?

10

Relational accompaniment: learning from the critics

Spelling out the challenges

Oliver James is a clinical psychologist who has written widely on human nurture. His book *Affluenza* offers a highly influential critique of contemporary Western society.[62] He is not, of course, addressing the rationale of Christian mission accompaniment specifically. He is, however, taking issue with some of the underlying insights and practices that we are commending for the accompaniment task.

'Affluenza' is a term that Oliver James uses to describe the symptoms of our culture's heightened anxiety about performance, image and achievement. (The term itself dates back several decades earlier.) In his book, James identifies an enervating ennui leading to inner despair. This, he says, characterises our culture. We want more; we can't have it. We reach higher; we can't get there. We collude with our own discontent. This in turn becomes a prevailing, all-pervading malaise, which comprises the 'affluenza' of the book's title.

We can identify three challenges in particular that are well made, and worthy of our attention, and to which we need to make considered response. They are:

- The unrealistic aspirations of the positive-thinking genre.
- The unwarranted pressure of pushing for greater performance.
- The short-sightedness of working with individuals without addressing the need for change in the larger systems of which they are part.

As practitioners of a Christian relational accompaniment, we want to be sure that we are modelling our practice on Jesus rather than the prevailing secular culture. We therefore welcome the challenge and accept the invitation to critique our assumptions and working practices. As genuine learners, and searchers for ever-clearer insight, we hold out the possibility that we might actually learn something fresh, modify our expectations and arrive somewhere even better.

Challenge one: positive thinking in cloud cuckoo land?

Thoughts are powerful. This insight is not unique to the self-help movement, but it is a basic assumption, and it is quite right. 'Above all else, guard your heart, for everything you do flows from it,' runs Proverbs 4:23. 'What goes into a person's mouth does not make them unclean,' says Jesus (Matthew 15:11). The Christian tradition has long understood the life-shaping effect of our innermost thoughts.

The contemporary multi-million-pound self-help movement has come a very long way since the publication of the book that gave it its name. *Self-Help* by Samuel Smiles was first published in 1859. The Wikipedia entry on the subject speaks now of an $11 billion industry. This is serious money, and it tells us that the need being addressed remains a serious issue for the human family.

The movement can rightly be critiqued for being more concerned with 'self' than with 'help'. It can be accused of being individualistic, narcissistic and self-obsessed. But its continued growth tells us something important. The industry continues to grow because nothing yet published answers the questions to our satisfaction. This is an itch that no amount of scratching has assuaged. We continue to feel dissatisfied with our lot, and we know that we could do better. We understand that our thoughts, our heart attitude and our inner dialogue are deeply enmeshed in the way that we experience life. But we can't quite grasp how to effect lasting, positive change. So we find ourselves susceptible to the offer of yet more esoteric insight. We are ready and willing to pay in order to continue our quest. We are, however, equally open to those who play on our insecurities, as to those who offer constructive insights.

Dipping into the bag

The positive-thinking oeuvre is a very mixed bag. Norman Vincent Peale was a Methodist minister. His work is replete with biblical quotation.[63] It can be accused of an overblown optimism, and a failure to take seriously the harsher realities, but it affirms a very well-founded truth. 'A reflective, contented mind is the best possession,' says Zoroaster. 'You are what you think. All that you are arises from your thoughts. With your thoughts you make your world,' says Buddha. 'A man is but the product of his thoughts. What he thinks, he becomes,' says Gandhi. 'Whatever is true, whatever is noble, whatever is right, whatever is pure, whatever is lovely, whatever is admirable – if anything is excellent or praiseworthy – think about such things,' says Paul (Philippians 4:8).

At the other end of the spectrum, *The Secret* by Rhonda Byrne reads like total nonsense: 'You can have what you want – if you know how to form the mould for it in your own thoughts. There is no dream that may not come true, if you but learn to use the creative force working through you.'[64]

The language and concepts of positive thinking have strongly influenced the discipline of life coaching. The accompanier will use the very best of its insights. There will be no change in the lives of our colleagues unless they review and work with their innermost thoughts. We will, however, need to position ourselves wisely on the spectrum. 'Believe in yourself. Have faith in your abilities,' says Norman Vincent Peale, and it sounds like perfectly good advice. 'Search me, God, and know my heart; test me and know my anxious thoughts,' says the psalmist (Psalm 139:23), and the mission accompanier will concur.

Oliver James suggests, however, that it is the raising of personal aspiration to an unrealistically high level that is a major source of discontent in the modern world. If we really can't have everything, then why are we encouraging people to want more? We are being unrealistic in raising unrealisable expectations, he says. But people do not live by bread alone, and Jesus promises life to the full. Wherever that fullness of life is not in evidence, then there is more to pursue.

Uncovering the roots of fear

As we have seen, our mission accompaniment will often take us into the territory of our colleagues' most deeply buried personal motivation. 'What do you actually want?' I ask a group of church leaders. Then, when they have outlined vague hopes for greater community contact, the ability to connect with missing population groups from their congregations and more robust financial underpinning, I ask again, 'What do you really want?' This time we move a little closer to some of the less-often disclosed personal motivations. 'To be seen to be doing a good job.' 'To be valued for my contributions.' 'To be accepted, appreciated, understood, loved.' And then, one final time, 'What do you really, really want?'

Jungian psychologist James Hollis says, 'Learning that fear governs our lives, and the many coping strategies we have evolved to manage it, may be an unpleasant discovery, but it is the beginning of liberation.'[65] Using the simple Jungian distinction between extroversion and introversion, Hollis proposes that ultimately extroverts fear abandonment and introverts fear being overwhelmed. These fears, hidden or acknowledged, will shape our lives and drive our behaviour until confronted, accepted and worked through. Even then, they are unlikely to disappear entirely. The accompanier will be a companion in facing up to these continuing realities.

Dorothy Rowe describes these twin threats as 'annihilation of the self'.[66] She relates an exercise, which she uses regularly with clients during her work as a psychologist, that she calls 'laddering'. She begins by asking what the source of her client's anxiety is. 'And why is that a threat?' 'What would happen to you, if that came to pass?' By asking again and again, the conversation slowly uncovers that basic, primal fear of annihilation. For the extrovert, it is abandonment. For the introvert, it is being overwhelmed.

Companions on the journey

Mission accompaniers are learning to journey with others on their quest for positive personal growth and fulfilment. We stand alongside our companions in the face of potentially overwhelming threats. Once again, it matters that we are clear about the goal towards which we are working.

We have a foundational belief, built upon that promise of Jesus, that life could be better than is currently experienced. Christian hope is so very much more than the avoidance of pain or the achievement of a particular personal goal. The ability to believe in, live for and pursue a better tomorrow is of the essence of a Christian's vocation. The mission accompanier is offering help, but it is more than self-help and it is pursuing more than simply surviving in the face of fear.

Challenge two: colluding with a materialistic driven culture?

How healthy anyway is our drive towards success and fulfilment? Coaching for enhanced performance, in the view of Oliver James, is part of the problem, not part of the solution. Christian mission accompaniers will want to hear this criticism and respond to this challenge.

In any work with colleagues in ministry, the accompanier will certainly want to ask, 'Am I simply being asked to push this person towards ever more productive performance?' 'Am I becoming part of the problem?' 'Could it be that I am piling up the pressure on an already overworked and under-resourced colleague?'

If we are genuinely to be part of the solution, we will need to take stock, listen to our critics and check our own motivation and integrity at this point also. We will want continually to monitor our working practices against a gospel perspective and the values of a flourishing life. We can therefore welcome this critique of our assumptions and ask again, 'How does this concur with or challenge what we have so far discovered?'

We have said:

Accompaniment is consistent engagement, with individuals or teams, for the greater flourishing of their lives and work. It will include elements of coaching, mentoring and simple friendship. It will reveal its greatest value as each of those elements is combined and transcended.

The principles and practices of accompaniment will be equally applicable at the start, the middle and the end of a journey of faith. They will make a significant contribution to discipling, to supporting ministry and to developing leadership roles. They will inform and enhance coaching, mentoring and indeed simple friendship. They will contribute to our flourishing in all that God has intended for us as friends and colleagues. They will make a difference for the kingdom of God.

Facing honest questions

We need to be absolutely clear that our motivation is shaped by a desire for human flourishing and not by any less worthy goal. Our commitment is to a theology of *imago Dei*. That means people reflecting and not distorting the image of God. Our values are those of Christian discipleship, and not a blind pursuit of material success. While we are happy to use the tools, our goals are different from those of a secular coaching model. The values, identity and passions that drive us have their origins and inspiration in the heart of God. God is relational. He calls us as friends. Our desire for enhanced performance is an outworking of our vocation to flourish, not a means to secure an identity or prove a point.

Testing ourselves against neo-liberalism

The underlying research for Oliver James' *Affluenza* is spelled out in greater detail in his subsequent book *The Selfish Capitalist*.[67] In this later work, James explains what he sees as the source of chronic discontent and heightened anxiety in 21st-century Western society. What he identifies is a deep-seated underlying approach to materialism on which this aspiration is based. This is particularly prevalent, he tells us, in the English-speaking world. This is what he calls 'neo-liberalism'.

Oliver James illustrates these developments by citing recent political trends. He describes the deregulation in financial markets, the prioritising of short-term share price over long-term investment and the privatisation of resources. These, he tells us, are potentially destructive of our well-being and are all founded on the discredited belief that unfettered materialism would promote well-being for all. He traces the roots of this thinking from Friedrich Hayek and Milton Friedman and shows how it has come down to us in the West as the trickle-down theory of 'Reaganomics' and 'Thatcherism'.

Hearing what we need to hear

Agreeing or not with the political critique is not actually the issue. What is unarguably true is that we, and many of our contemporaries, now live under increasing pressure to meet ever greater demands. This is currently the way of the world, and is true whether we are in education, healthcare or business. Those whom we accompany in church life are not immune.

Belgian psychologist Paul Verhaeghe ascribes the rise of burnout and depression to the increasing pressure on individuals to behave and be treated as units of production and consumption rather than as human beings in social relationship with one another.[68]

This view of the world suggests that, in seeking to develop the performance of individuals, we are colluding with those pressures. Coaching for performance can be taken captive by a materialistic view of the world. Accompaniers take note, and let's be sure to keep our focus on the relational flourishing that Jesus promises, life and life to the full.

More rubber, more road

I am sitting in a battered leather armchair. A small fire is flickering in the grate, making very little headway in combating the room's chilly atmosphere. Across from me sit the Area Dean and his colleague, the Lay Chairman. Their deanery is struggling, both financially and missionally. Neither could be said to be flourishing. I am, at that moment, their deanery mission accompanier. Burnout and depression are crouching at the door, not yet devouring, but seriously ready to pounce. One of the background voices in my mind is that of the Archdeacon: 'They have simply got to find a way to turn things around, otherwise I don't know what will happen.' (My compassion for the Archdeacon ratchets up, and I wonder just what flourishing would look like for him right now.) Back in the chilly room, I prepare to frame my next question. Will I collude with their negativity? Or am I expected to offer them a simple solution? Should I challenge their level of faith and stir in some positivity? What am I there for? What will godly flourishing look like in the face of these very real, and seemingly insurmountable, pressures? I will listen again to the critics before responding and running the risk of adding to their burdens.

Weighing the next move

To build an appropriate response to my beleaguered colleagues, it will be vital to remind myself of our shared discipleship values. Here, more than anywhere, I need to resist any other agenda. The bottom line for us here is not financial. We are not driven by outcomes to be measured simply in numbers. For us in this conversation, our goals will not be measured in promotions gained or targets met.

Of course, in the reality of our context, these things do matter. We cannot escape the truth that we are part of an organisation in which, for the moment, buildings need to be maintained, books need to balance and change needs to be managed. But they are not (or should not be) determinative. We can be clear that relational flourishing is our highest value and that integrity of purpose and quality of life are our supreme measures. We remind ourselves that if gospel mission is at heart relational, then how on earth could we expect to promote that mission while at the same time allowing relational damage to those who pursue it?

Whatever my next words, they will be founded upon an existing relational engagement. They will take seriously just what my colleagues are experiencing at this moment and they will assure an ongoing commitment to whatever the future holds.

'What was it that really excited you the most, about this role, when you first took it on?' I ask. In that moment, the starting point of the conversation shifts. Briefly, we move focus from the current overwhelming difficulties to the much more motivating area of vocation. Here, we hope to find the source of creative energy that will ultimately provide the motivation in moving forward. 'Let's talk for a while about what really fires you up!'

There is one more critique that demands a response. It takes us beyond the personal and into the arena of corporate culture.

Challenge three: addressing individuals while ignoring context?

Oliver James is particularly critical of cognitive behavioural therapy (CBT). (Like coaching and NLP, this is a tool for addressing underlying thought patterns and their consequences.) He is dismissive of what he sees as its pretentions to quick fix. He is suspicious of its use as a tool for addressing the individual's response to unwarranted pressures rather than addressing the source of the pressures themselves. He interprets it rather like the patching up of wounded soldiers, only to send them back into the senseless and uneven conflict that caused them injury in the first place. This challenge matters to us as accompaniers, because much of our coaching theory and many of our NLP tools draw from the same underlying assumptions as CBT.

Challenging the context

Put simply, is accompaniment solely concerned with the individual while ignoring the wider system of which they are a part?

Driving through the deanery, mile after mile, village after village, parish after parish, you cannot but be momentarily overwhelmed by the size of the task. Here are three villages, each of which within living memory had its own vicar in its own vicarage, now working together with one full-time clergyperson between them. Now they are being told they will have to combine with a fourth. Who knows how long before a fifth or a sixth is added? Is mission accompaniment in such a setting simply a case of trying to increase the resilience of the one now bearing the burden? Are we looking to strengthen the arms and broaden the shoulders only? Or can we address the wider context, and try to change the way in which it is perceived, understood and responded to?

It is certainly true that individual accompaniment sessions are most effective when focused on areas within the individual's own sphere of influence. 'What can you do? What could you do? What will you do?' Accompaniment will, on most occasions, start there. Honest and constructive answers to those questions will, though, soon lead into reflection on wider context. 'What are the constraints? Which factors lie completely outside your orbit of influence and which within it?' 'What does faith-inspired, hope-informed, kingdom of God-shaped leadership look like here?' The accompanier does not need to have, indeed could not be expected to have, all the answers, but appropriate questions will move the conversation beyond simply trying to encourage the colleague to have a more positive outlook on life.

The conversation will eventually move on from personal resilience to social and cultural factors. Beyond that again lie the people questions: 'Who are your partners in this? Who could make a difference? With whom could you share your perspective, and from whom could you invite a response?' Before very long, this is a conversation with profound implications up and down the line. Fellow church leaders, colleagues in neighbouring churches, ecumenical partners, community leaders, parishioners, schools, police, social services, businesses, all become players in the drama of aspiration towards community flourishing. Mission accompaniment, while being at heart a one-on-one skill, simply cannot avoid the wider context in which it is set. The environment in which a church, deanery or diocese engages in accompaniment lifts it out of the individualistic and into the corporate.

As for the Canterbury narrative described earlier, it was an underlying concern for culture change that helped to shape the accompaniment programme. Working with and supporting individuals soon led to the realisation that a flourishing diocese will largely be an outworking of flourishing individuals, in healthy relationship with each other. A serious attempt to change culture has profound implications both for individuals and for the context of which they are a part.

Summarising lessons from the critics

Paying over much heed to the wilder end of the positive-thinking genre can indeed lead to a selfish obsession with our own success. Buying into neo-liberal political assumptions may end up commodifying individuals and serving the greed of a dominating elite and the institutions that protect them. Pursuing a coaching model that deals purely with individuals and their own motivation may lead to an avoidance of the much greater complexity in the structure of the system itself. All these are valid observations, and all are worth pondering by the dedicated accompanier. But none of those criticisms strike a fatal blow at the concept of relational accompaniment per se, rooted as it is in a relational God calling relational individuals into a community of relational flourishing, in which the promise of life still holds.

Your personal reflection

- What hidden fears hold you back from pursuing positive, meaningful change?

11

Relational accompaniment: applying the principles

Accompaniment is consistent engagement, with individuals or teams, for the greater flourishing of their lives and work. It will include elements of coaching, mentoring and simple friendship. It will reveal its greatest value as each of those elements is combined and transcended.

The principles and practices of accompaniment will be equally applicable at the start, the middle and the end of a journey of faith. They will make a significant contribution to discipling, to supporting ministry and to developing leadership roles. They will inform and enhance coaching, mentoring and indeed simple friendship. They will contribute to our flourishing in all that God has intended for us as friends and colleagues. They will make a difference for the kingdom of God.

Five points of the star

It should be clear by now that relational accompaniment is a life skill rather than a technique. Our effectiveness as accompaniers will flow, to the greatest extent, from our own flourishing. It is an art more than a science. Our own growth, our own positive, healthy, adult-to-adult relationships will provide the basis for what we bring to the task. There are, however, some simple, summarising headings that can be laid out. This chapter is the nearest we get to instructions of the self-assembly-furniture variety (insert flange A into slot B, then turn screw C).

These are not 'rules', they do not form an agenda, but they describe the basic shape of accompaniment. Let's call it a star with five points.

Diagram 5: Five-pointed star

1   Agree the terms of engagement.
2   Stop. Look. Listen.
3   Ask elucidating questions.
4   Hone specific outcomes.
5   Hold to account.

At the core of the star is our relational God. This is always the beating heart of what we are about. This is the theological foundation, upon which is built our self-understanding of relational human beings called into the matrix of relational church to make a difference in the world.

From here, we draw on all that we have gleaned from the aspirational searching of our species. Coaching skills, positive volition, tools and techniques for marshalling our wayward thoughts, addressing our hidden fears, revealing our vague hopes and uncovering our buried longing are all called into service.

The points of the star will always feature, in some shape or form, within every accompaniment journey.

Agree the terms of engagement

Not every accompaniment will be a formally contracted engagement, but some will. We need to be aware of the difference, and frame our relationships accordingly. In the case of accompanying a pioneer or team through the early days of a new project, a more formal protocol will be agreed, preferably in writing. 'We will meet for 90 minutes, once a month, for the next year and a half,' for example.

Accompanied deaneries in the Canterbury Diocese commit to a schedule outlined on one side of A4. It covers frequency of meetings and which gatherings the accompanier will attend, in addition to the core programme and parameters of responsibility. It emphasises that local mission remains in the hands of local churches, and the accompanier accompanies, nothing more.

Working one-to-one with new or potential disciples, the parameters are less formal but need to be equally clear. 'How about meeting for coffee once a fortnight?' we might say. 'How would it be if we were to catch up with each other regularly, over the next three months? Would you find that helpful, do you think?' If this is genuinely relational, then it will be shaped by the response given and the level of engagement desired.

Using accompaniment insights to enhance ongoing friendships is yet another matter. Even more interesting is when it forms part of family banter. A wry smile plays on the lips of family members, or close friends, whenever I say, 'Do you mind if I ask you a question?' At least I've remembered to get permission!

Stop. Look. Listen.

This is second nature to anybody trained in counselling or supportive ministries of any kind. But it is surprisingly easy to slip out of, thinking it to be essentially a pastoral skill only. In the early days of deliberately using accompaniment protocols, I was often having to remind myself to stop framing clever responses, listen intently and ask yet more questions.

If, however, the non-directive approach is overplayed, it can become rather irritating for the colleague with whom you are working. There are times when advice is specifically sought. In response to a specific request for information or advice, I will regularly say, 'I will let you know what I think in a moment. Can we be sure that we have heard all that you have to say, first?' That, for me, is one classic distinction between accompanier and mentor. Whenever I offer specific insight or information, I make it clear that, in that moment, I am changing role from the one to the other.

Ask elucidating questions

I still cherish the look on my colleague's face when I asked him about his body mass index. We had been talking specifically about personal flourishing and how an all-pervading sense of lethargy was currently hampering his ability to make good decisions. I have been surprised to discover how many of my friends describe the feelings of exhilaration that they experience when out running. It turned out that this man too was a runner, or had been in times past. The right choice of question opened up a whole new area to explore. New commitments were made, and life began to change for the better.

I would not dream of telling a client, or a friend for that matter, that they need to take more exercise. That's not my place. But, as a contribution to conversation started in answer to an innocent question, I often tell my story. I do 50 press-ups in the morning, have twice-weekly visits to the gym, and complete 20-minute sessions on the cross-country ski machine; these are all components of my own mood management. The resultant physical well-being is a bonus. The questions we ask and the stories we tell in accompaniment do not have to focus entirely on work.

The intention of our questions is to stimulate further insight. For that reason, our ability to delve gently into hidden motivations is a premium skill. 'Why do you think that matters to you so much?' we ask. 'What does that remind you of?' (Sometimes you need a box of tissues to hand.)

Hone specific outcomes

Of all the skills acquired and techniques employed, this is probably the single most essential component to lift accompaniment out of the mundane and familiar and into the realms of effective change and breakthrough. This is not something that we normally do. It makes a difference. I love it when the lights go on in the eyes of a client or friend. 'You know what? I'm going to invite her out for coffee and listen to her story. I'll tell her what I'm going through and how I feel. It may not make any difference, but I'll know that she knows, and it may just change our working relationship.' I wasn't pressing, or forcing the pace; my colleague simply had a moment of breakthrough insight and committed herself to a specific course of action. She knew and articulated exactly what she would do next. This was her goal, her outcome, and it was shaped precisely. The only remaining question for me to ask was, 'When exactly will you do that?'

Hold to account

'I knew you were going to ask that,' says a colleague, with a grin. We had agreed in our previous conversation that he would read a particular book. This is a young pioneer minister, energetic, outgoing and highly active. He is not a natural reader. But he had exhausted his own instinctive approaches to a specific piece of work. There is a wealth of information, a fund of stories and stimulating insight to be discovered in the writings of other pioneers. We talked about it. I had certainly not told him he should read up on it. That was his own idea. We had engaged in the exercise of asking, 'What could you do?', and 'What more could you do?' He had identified the possibility of reading, and had asked for suggestions. *Being Church; Doing Life* by Michael Moynagh was top of my list at the time.[69] When it came to clarifying the outcomes of our session, he committed himself to making a start on the book before we next met.

Of course, I was going to ask if he had fulfilled his resolve. That's how accompaniment works. But these were early days and he was only just grasping the significance of the process. In fact, next time we met, he had only picked up the book, for the first time, the previous evening. He had belatedly realised that I was going to ask that very question. The point is not that he should feel guilty for letting me down. It is that he will grow into the realisation that when he commits to doing something, he will see it through. The book, incidentally, proved of sufficient value for him to continue reading out of his own passion and desire to learn more. The motivation came from within. The accountability component of accompaniment had played its part.

In summary

One star, five points. God, and the relational accompaniment that he offers to us, at the heart. A cluster of skills and insights around that heart. Five specific components that will take us beyond hoping for the best, beyond simply 'being there', and into the realms of life-shaping culture change.

Time now, in the final chapter, to do what all good accompaniment should aim for: now to clarify our own outcomes. When we commit ourselves to the route of accompaniment, what ultimately are we hoping to achieve? What will this look like, feel like, taste like, in the real world of our everyday experience? How does it shape our Christian journey?

Your personal reflection

- Which of those five star points comes most naturally to you?
- Which requires most attention and honing, for you to use it well?
- What difference would the application of those principles make in the ongoing support that you receive from and offer to others?

12

Towards the goal of relational accompaniment

Refocusing the goal

What, in the grand scheme of things, is all our relational accompaniment aiming to achieve? What is our big-picture outcome? What is our deepest-seated motivating vision?

When I am sitting in a diocesan office, meeting with the bishop and their team, then a viable financial and missional strategy would be a great outcome of our work. Or if we are in an area dean's study, then a fresh vision for the deanery, a manageable workload for local clergy and a tiny upturn in numbers would be just fine. Maybe this is an engagement with a newly appointed pioneer, in which case we're looking for a clear grasp of expectations. In every case, we want to discover what is genuinely possible. And if this is a one-to-one conversation with a friend on their journey through life, then the reordering of muddled thoughts and the identification of next steps would be more than satisfactory. At every point, there are specific strategic measurable outcomes that shape our engagement.

But there is more. Always, there is very much more.

Stephen R. Covey talks of 'synergy'. There is something mysterious, mystical even, that lies beyond all the applied pragmatic wisdom of his advice. 'When properly understood, synergy is the highest activity in all life – the true test and manifestation of all the other habits put together.'[70] He is not the only one to get excited by this captivating possibility.

M. Scott Peck uses the term 'community'.[71] After all his years of medical and psychiatric work, after all his multiple psychological publications, this was what he pursued in the final years of his life. 'In and through community lies the salvation of the world. Nothing is more important.'[72] Peck describes the spine-tingling moments when a disparate group of people finally break through into genuine community.

Some time earlier, Jesus put it this way: 'A new command I give you: love one another' (John 13:34).

Synergy. Community. Love. There is a great, grand goal, way beyond the search for increased efficiency. There is a longer-term, higher-order aspiration at work which goes miles beyond ticking boxes and fulfilling tasks. To quote Scott Peck again, 'Community-building first, problem-solving second'.[73]

This is our calling: the relational church of a relational God seeking to live its mission, incarnate its vocation and anticipate its destiny. This is about people flourishing as people, and doing it together. It is a recognition of the value and sacredness of the individual, expressed in community and lived in context. It is about acceptance and accepting, support and supporting, encouragement and encouraging as the core values of a new kingdom.

We are where we are

So, here's a question. How is it that writers such as Stephen Covey and Scott Peck can portray supportive, synergistic, loving community relationships as if this were a previously unimagined goal? Why does it sound so enticing, so energising and so unfamiliar on their lips? Has it not, all along, been the prime vocation of the Christian church? How could we have so failed in our calling that a restatement of central Christian values now sounds like a totally fresh revelation? How could we have found ourselves in a situation where the foundational components of Christ's kingdom sound like a breakthrough of contemporary sociological and psychological insight? But that is undoubtedly where we are.

It is this perceived lack of foundational engagement that Steve Aisthorpe uncovered in his research published as *The Invisible Church*, quoted in chapter 4. In Aisthorpe's chapter 8, 'Learning to love', he describes the simple but profoundly overwhelming insight that it is a felt lack of love that eventually drives many from our churches, and prevents very many others from joining in the first place. All the growth strategies in the world, all the fresh pioneering initiatives and even all the calls to prayer will be of little lasting effect if the foundational one-to-one engagements do not reflect and embody the relational nature of a relational God. Let us be absolutely frank: the long-term outcomes of the current (perfectly understandable) emphasis on more highly skilled, strategic change management in the upper echelons of the church will depend almost entirely upon the quality of the personal relationships at their heart.

It's what friends are for

Most of us will not be in a position to found a company, lead a diocese or even be employed as a professional mission accompanier. Does that mean that we cannot contribute towards the flourishing of those around us? Are we unable to influence and help effect a culture change? Not a bit; in fact, if anything like a deep-seated culture change is to take root in any context, it will require a willing participation at the level of ordinary everyday human interaction. It will be up to us.

Jean (not her real name) had been coming along quite regularly to the Messy Church event hosted in her village hall. She was a very clear example of what the leaders of that work described as 'people that we have been highly successful in reaching, but simply can't get to attend our regular Sunday worship'. 'It's the obvious next step,' they said, 'but we simply don't know how to achieve it.' Was it so obvious? Certainly not to Jean herself, and if that was how she saw it, then they were going to have to think again. In their own accompaniment, those Messy Church team leaders were encouraged to rethink their approach. What if it was the simple, interactive, relational approach of their event that was attractive to Jean? What if Sunday worship, as presently conducted, was never going to be the location of her next steps in Christian discipleship?

Further questioning revealed that Jean had been invited in the first instance by Julie, not herself part of the regular Messy Church team, but a fairly consistent member of the local congregation nonetheless. Julie was not trained in any kind of 'discipleship programme'; she had never led a Bible study or taught a Sunday-school class. But she had been motivated enough, perhaps out of simple friendship, to invite Jean to come with her and her children to the event in the village hall.

At this point, the team was beginning to sense possibilities. It did not take long, though, for the next level of objections to surface. 'We can't ask Julie to set up a group, even if it isn't a Bible study. Actually, we don't really know how mature Julie is in her own faith. I'm not sure we could ask her to take any responsibility.' I can imagine this same conversation, or one very much like it, taking place over and over again, and not only in Messy Church contexts. Wherever a group of Christians are reaching out to neighbours, they are likely to find a level of responsiveness that gives great encouragement, but stops short of their new friends wanting to join them in church on Sunday.

'How did Jesus go about helping his friends to pursue their faith journey?' I ask that team. After the more obvious headline-grabbing stories of leaving nets and listening to sermons in boats or on mountainsides, we find ourselves revisiting Luke's Gospel. Chapter 7 shows Jesus hanging out, eating and drinking with groups of casual acquaintances. Chapter 8 tells of some of those same people now walking and talking with him, and each other, as they set out on a journey. No doubt they are swapping stories, building friendships where only passing acknowledgement had previously existed. Few of them would even have been able to articulate their own beliefs at this stage, but a journey had begun. It is only much later, in chapter 10, that Jesus sets them a task, as they are sent out, two by two, in a more challenging participation in the mission of the kingdom. Even at this stage, convictions would be half-formed and unclear, but that doesn't seem to matter. Relationships come first, and not only as a prelude to being set a task, but because relationships matter in themselves. They are the stuff of God's kingdom.

Pennies are dropping as we explore together what this might look like in the context of Messy Church in general, and the question of encouraging Jean in particular. 'Maybe we don't need any other event at all, at this stage. After all, we sit at table together during our Messy Church, and not just when we're eating. What if one of us were to sit with Jean and Julie? What if others were invited to join us? What if we gave some time just to tell our stories to each other while the rest are colouring, baking and playing? It wouldn't have to be Bible study, but it could certainly include life-shaped, faith sharing.'

Friends indeed?

Who knows for sure whether the catechumenate of the early church did not begin in such an unstructured friendship-based way? We know from the writings of Justin Martyr in the second century that, by then, Christian disciples were being instructed in a formal way prior to baptism, usually at Easter. We know that, down the centuries, Christian 'learners' (disciples) have been helped on their faith journey by those who have travelled the path before them. What we do not know is how much early accompaniment took place, simply from one believer to another, one learner to another, one disciple to another. It could have been a very great deal. Perhaps that is essentially the way in which the early church grew so far, so fast.

Motivational speaker Paul McGee styles himself as 'the SUMO guy'. The acronym stands for 'shut up and move on'! McGee's book *Self-Confidence* reached number one on the W.H. Smith business books list.[74] Chapter 5 of that book is titled, somewhat counter-intuitively, 'A little help from your friends'. He outlines four specific roles that one should look for in supportive friendships: Challenger, Cheerleader, Confidant and Coach. The actual roles are fairly self-explanatory. What he goes on to say, though, is that you are unlikely to find all those roles in your current circle and specifically not combined in one person. But what if we were to rise to the challenge? What if we saw the value of providing that for each other? What if we sought to develop those specific gifts and skills in order to enhance the life experience of those around us? What if…?

And in conclusion

Winston Churchill described the art of listening as an act of courage. Bryant McGill calls it a mark of respect. 'Being heard is so close to being loved that for the average person, they are almost indistinguishable,' writes American Anabaptist David Augsburger.[75]

An accompanier gives the gift of attention. To be paid attention to, taken seriously and heard without interruption is a gift of grace. Being there consistently, listening attentively and engaging judiciously are the hallmarks of great friendship. Honed accompaniment will add the vital components, outlined here, that can effect lasting change.

Will this kind of accompaniment halt decline, fill churches and balance books? Will it reverse the graphs and turn around the fortunes of institutional Christianity? We simply don't know the answer to that. The multiple factors that contribute to the mystifying complexity of contemporary society are unlikely to melt away in the face of one fresh emphasis. What we can say, though, is that this approach looks very much like adopting the right values for the right reasons at the right time. It seems to reveal God's heart, and experience suggests that is the only place to expect to find the source of real flourishing.

Accompaniment allows us to grasp the foundational theological insight, that God is relational. It allows us to invite the whole of humanity to a relational journey, and to build a model and a practice around that. It places stimulating engagement, mutual support and a passion for human flourishing firmly at the top of our agenda. It releases us to pursue godly growth in human and personal terms. It allows us to put first things first.

If God is relational, if human beings bearing his image are fundamentally relational, if mission is relational, then a theology, model and practice shaped relationally will be the only way to live with integrity. Such is accompaniment. Applied consistently, it could change a culture.

The concluding challenge

- What has this clarified for you?
- What questions remain?
- What will you now do with all that you have read here?

Be specific. Be honest about the realities. Review your options. Act. Perhaps find someone to accompany you on the next stage of the journey. Ask who might appreciate your companionship as you offer accompaniment to them. Find a friend. Be a friend. Change the world.

Notes

1 William James, *The Letters of William James*, ed. Henry James (1926), vol. 2, p. 90.
2 *Mission-Shaped Church* (Church House Publishing, 2004).
3 *Gilgamesh Epic* (Penguin Classics, 1999).
4 J.R.R. Tolkien, *The Lord of the Rings* (George Allen & Unwin, 1968).
5 Dan Siegel, *Mind: A journey to the heart of being human* (W.W. Norton, 2017).
6 Laura Berman Fortgang, *Take Yourself to the Top* (Warner Books, 1998).
7 Huw Thomas and Martyn Snow, *Coaching in the Church* (Grove Books – Pastoral Series 115, 2008).
8 Terry Tennens (ed.), *Journey into Growth* (Churches Together in Britain and Ireland, 2007).
9 See the story more fully in chapter 4, 'Relational church'.
10 Karen Armstrong, *A Short History of Myth* (Canongate, 2005).
11 Alexander Eliot, *The Universal Myths* (Truman Talley, 1976).
12 Lesslie Newbiggin, *The Household of God* (Paternoster Press, 1998), p. 24.
13 Walter Brueggemann, *Genesis* (Westminster John Knox Press, 1982).
14 G.E. Ladd, *A Theology of the New Testament* (Eerdmans, 1974), p. 58.
15 Paul Tournier, *The Meaning of Persons* (SCM, 1957), p. 73.
16 Martin Buber, *I and Thou* (T&T Clark, 1958), p. 25.
17 Dan Siegel, *The Developing Mind* (Guilford Press, 1999).
18 Eric Berne, *Games People Play* (Penguin Books, 1964).
19 M. David Enoch, *Healing the Hurt Mind* (Hodder & Stoughton, 1983).
20 Guy Chevreau, *Catch the Fire* (Marshall Pickering, 1994).
21 Alain de Botton, *Religion for Atheists* (Penguin, 2012).
22 The Centre for Economic Policy Research, *The Origins of Happiness* (Princeton University Press, 2016).
23 Michael Moynagh, *Church for Every Context* (SCM, 2012).
24 *Mission-Shaped Church* (Church House Publishing, 2004).
25 Jürgen Moltmann, *The Open Church* (SCM, 1978).
26 Jürgen Moltmann, *The Church in the Power of the Spirit* (SCM, 1977).
27 Jürgen Moltmann, *The Living God and Fullness of Life* (Westminster John Knox Press, 2015).

28   Moltmann, *The Living God*, p. 27, p. 32, respectively.
29   Moltmann, *The Living God*, p. 32.
30   Christian Schwarz, *Natural Church Development: A practical guide to a new approach* (The British Church Growth Association, 1996).
31   Quoted by Steve Aisthorpe in *The Invisible Church* (Saint Andrew Press, 2016).
32   Aisthorpe, *The Invisible Church*, p. 153.
33   See Phil Potter, *The Challenge of Cell Church* (BRF, 2001).
34   Mike Breen and Walt Kallestad, *A Passionate Life* (NexGen, 2005).
35   John Whitmore, *Coaching for Performance* (Nicholas Brealey, 1992).
36   Myles Downey, *Effective Coaching* (Orion, 1999).
37   Nancy Kline, *Time to Think* (Cassell, 1999).
38   Stephen R. Covey, *The 7 Habits of Highly Effective People* (Simon & Schuster, 1989), p. 53.
39   M. Scott Peck, *The Road Less Travelled* (Simon & Schuster, 1978).
40   Norman Vincent Peale, *The Power of Positive Thinking* (The World's Work, 1953).
41   Steve Bavister and Amanda Vickers, *Teach Yourself NLP* (2004), p. 2, p. 13, respectively.
42   Visit the NLP School, **www.nlpschool.com**, for a particularly self-aware, relaxed approach to the studies.
43   John Grinder and Richard Bandler, *The Structure of Magic* (Science and Behaviour Books, 1975).
44   Available online: Robert Dilts, *A Brief History of Logical Levels*.
45   George New and David Cormack, *Why Did I Do That?* (Hodder & Stoughton, 1997).
46   Frederick Herzberg, *One More Time: How do you motivate employees?* (1978; Harvard Business Review Classics, 2008).
47   Tom Wright, *Virtue Reborn* (SPCK, 2010), p. 1.
48   Steve Peters, *The Chimp Paradox* (Vermillion, 2012).
49   Viktor Frankl, *Man's Search for Meaning* (Washington Square Press, 1984), p. 126.
50   Vincent Donovan, *Christianity Rediscovered* (SCM Classics, 2001; originally published by Orbis, 1978).
51   Bob Hopkins and Freddy Hedley, *Coaching for Missional Leadership* (ACPI, 2008).
52   Hopkins and Hedley, *Coaching for Missional Leadership* (Kindle edition).
53   *Bishop's Mission Orders: A beginner's guide* (Church House Publishing, 2008).

54   Terry Tennens, *Journey into Growth* (CTBI, 2007).

55   Tennens, *Journey into Growth*, p. 7.

56   Philip Walker, *Mission Accompaniment* (Grove Books – Evangelism series 69, 2005).

57   Walker, *Mission Accompaniment*, p. 26.

58   Frederic Laloux, *Reinventing Organizations* (Nelson Parker, 2014).

59   Laloux, *Reinventing Organizations*, p. 238.

60   Laloux, *Reinventing Organizations*, p. 67.

61   Laloux, *Reinventing Organizations*, p. 219.

62   Oliver James, *Affluenza* (Vermillion, 2007). This title has sold over 150,000 copies.

63   Peale, *The Power of Positive Thinking*.

64   Rhonda Byrne, *The Secret* (Atria Books, 2006), p. 50.

65   James Hollis, *What Matters Most* (Gotham Books, 2009), p. 11.

66   Dorothy Rowe, *The Successful Self* (Harper Collins, 1993), p. 24.

67   Oliver James, *The Selfish Capitalist* (Vermillion, 2008).

68   Paul Verhaeghe, *What About Me?: The struggle for identity in a market-based society* (Scribe UK, 2014), translated by Jane Hedley-Prole.

69   Michael Moynagh, *Being Church; Doing Life* (Monarch, 2014).

70   Covey, *The 7 Habits of Highly Effective People*, p. 262.

71   M. Scott Peck, *The Different Drum* (Arrow Books, 1990).

72   Peck, *The Different Drum*, p. 17.

73   Peck, *The Different Drum*, p. 104.

74   Paul McGee, *Self-Confidence* (Capstone Publishing, 2010).

75   David Augsburger, *Caring Enough to Hear and Be Heard* (Herald Press, 1982), p. 12. Augsburger is Professor of Pastoral Counselling at Fuller Theological Seminary.

Transforming
lives and communities

Christian growth and understanding of the Bible

Resourcing individuals, groups and leaders in churches for their own spiritual journey and for their ministry

Church outreach in the local community

Offering three programmes that churches are embracing to great effect as they seek to engage with their local communities and transform lives

Teaching Christianity in primary schools

Working with children and teachers to explore Christianity creatively and confidently

Children's and family ministry

Working with churches and families to explore Christianity creatively and bring the Bible alive

Visit **brf.org.uk** for more information on BRF's work

brf.org.uk

The Bible Reading Fellowship (BRF) is a Registered Charity (No. 233280)